Floyd L. Ruff 3/28 09

Legacy to Legend: Winners *Make It* Happen

The Autobiography of

Floyd L. Griffin, Jr.

A Trailblazer

Student Civil Rights Activist
Helicopter Pilot in Vietnam
US Army Colonel
Georgia State Senator
Mayor of Milledgeville, GA
Businessman

Published By: Publishing Associates, Inc.
5020 Montcalm Drive
Atlanta, GA 30331
fcpublish@aol.com

ISBN: 978-0-942683-22-6

Legacy to Legend: Winners *Make It* Happen

The Autobiography of

Floyd L. Griffin, Jr.

A Trailblazer

Publishing Associates, Inc.
Atlanta, GA 30331

Table of Contents

Dedication

This book is dedicated to Nathalie Huffman Griffin
My loving and devoted wife.
Nathalie, as my life partner,
You have stood beside me in everything that I attempted
and stepped up to the plate whenever necessary.
You have put up with all my eccentricities and
loved me just the same.
You gave me strength when I thought I couldn't go on;
Perseverance when I wanted to give up;
Faith when I didn't want to believe in myself;
Hope when I thought all hope was gone;
Love when I thought I was unlovable.
We have been through college, the civil rights movement, protests, graduation, 42 years of marriage, 2 sons, 6 grandchildren, 14 moves, to enjoy enriching careers in the military, politics and in business.
My feelings for you have never changed;
I can't live without you

To my sons Eric and Brian
You have shown such perseverance and strength
throughout the years.
It comes as no surprise to me that you have succeeded in your
endeavors
A man couldn't ask for two better sons. I'm proud of you.
To my parents, the late Floyd L. Griffin, Sr. and
Ruth Evans Griffin
Daddy, you were such a tremendous role model
I know that you can see me and I hope I've done you proud
You showed me what it means to be a man of integrity
Everything that I am, I learned from you, I miss you.

Mom, for your love and support throughout the years
For being the strong woman behind Daddy
For being the loving presence that held it all together
Thank you
To my six grandchildren
Jamal, Brandon, Bacari, Braxton, Zac, and AnnaGail
Keep the legacy and the legend alive.
Remember: Winners Make It Happen

Acknowledgements

I wish to extend a word of recognition to the following persons who have been instrumental to my growth and development during different stages of my life. I'd like to thank Dr. P.B. Phillips, Dean of Students, Tuskegee Institute, Tuskegee, Alabama who during my days there as a college student was a courageous and unselfish organizer of Tuskegee Institute Community Education Program (TICEP). The program which grew to nearly 600 students was a major student resistance and support group serving the rural poor of Alabama during the Civil Rights era.

Role models, mentors and friends who inspired me during my military career were: Lt. General Joe Ballard, (Southern University), [the first African American Chief of the U.S. Army Corps of Engineers], Major General Charles Williams, (Tuskegee Institute [University]) and Major General Ernest Harrell (Tuskegee Institute [University]), Colonel William L. Mazyck, (South Carolina State University) and Lieutenant Colonel Ted Nell (South Carolina State University).

As a Politician among my many colleagues for change in the legislature and Civil Rights I'd like to thank the following persons: Georgia Senator Robert Brown and State Representative Tyrone Brooks. I'd like to also thank Leon Mitchell, my campaign manager during political campaigns for offices in the Senate, for Lieutenant Governor and Mayor. Other critical strategists and supporters of my campaigns were Beverly Calhoun, Julia Ingram, Annie Miller, Alice Mitchell, Doris Watson, and Margaret Hitchcock, my New York fundraiser and Milledgeville native. The person that became my scheduling and organization magnet throughout my political career was my executive assistant Joann Lunsford. I am grateful for her professionalism and attention to detail.

Finally, I 'd like to thank Amanda Smith of Macon, Georgia for her assisting me in organizing and drafting Part II - The Political Years- and working with my publisher in editing my memoirs.

Foreword

Floyd "Griff" Griffin:
My Army Comrade and Trusted Confidant
by Ted Nell, Lt. Col., U.S. Army (Retired)

I had the pleasure of meeting Floyd while performing military duties in Fort Benning, Georgia. In his capacity as a staff officer assigned to Fort Bragg, North Carolina, he travelled to Benning on official military duties; however, he also took time to attend a Saturday morning meeting of the Association of Modern Minority Officers (AMMO). The meeting's settings were unique to both of us because AMMO, a newly formed organization sanctioned by the installation's military authorities, was founded to address the diversity issues and concerns among the Army's officer corps. Our chance meeting on that occasion prompted me to get to know Floyd better because he immediately struck me as an extremely dedicated, focused, and caring professional.

My next visit with Floyd occurred at Fort Bragg, N.C. where he and his lovely wife Nathalie immediately designated themselves our unofficial sponsors because Floyd, a very perceptive and observant person, knew that I wasn't familiar with the Bragg community. My wife Shirley and I called upon the Griffins for assistance and advice not only during our relocation to the area, but during our entire tour there because we shared common interests, but more importantly knew that we could depend upon and trust them.

Floyd, who by this time had become my buddy Griff, and I cemented our relations as comrades in arms during our tours at Bragg, an elite Army post. Although his official military duties at Bragg kept him extremely busy, he never shied away from other challenging venues. Our fellow comrades unanimously selected him as the first President of the Interested Officers' Association (IOA), an organization founded with similar purposes and goals adopted by AMMO. Griff was propelled into the position as the organization's leader because the officer community at Bragg, minority and white alike, recognized him as a model officer who possessed the proper attitude and skills to represent minority positions. Griff's destiny to greater heights was recognized not only by the military community, but also by prominent civilians in the community and nationwide. Joe Frazier, former Heavyweight Boxing Champion of the World, remarked during a well attended IOA function, "This officer will be an Army General one day!" I believe that Griff's conscious decision to put his family first rather than furthering military service in an overseas assignment during his final military assignment precluded the realization of Frazier's prediction, one held by Griff's senior officers and contemporaries as well.

I marveled at Griff's ability to tackle a variety of tasks while continuing to excel in his assigned duties when Griff was reassigned from Bragg to duties as Assistant Professor of Military Science at Wake Forest University, North Carolina. His commitment to diversity among the Army's officer corps led him to establish a cross-enrollment Reserve Officers Training Corps (ROTC) program at Winston-Salem University (WSSU), a Historically Black College and University (HBCU). He masterfully handled his professional obligations while also volunteering his services as Backfield Coach for WSSU's football team which won Championships in the Central Intercollegiate Athletic Association (CIAA) two consecutive seasons.

A few years later, our families reunited when Griff and I were students at the Command & General Staff College (CGSC) in Fort Leavenworth, Kansas. Given the nature of this assignment away from the normal rigors and demands of management and leadership positions associated with the Army's war-fighting posture, Griff relished in the opportunity to spend more time with his family. He spent a great deal of non-student time strengthening bonds with his sons Brian and Eric as the Head Coach for their football teams, and he also supported them in student and other sports activities. Griff also eagerly looked forward to having quiet dinners and outings with his wife, fellow classmates and our spouses. Notwithstanding his familial priorities, he was called upon and drafted to become the President of our informal CGSC Minority Officers group, the formation which was yet another first for our officer contemporaries. Griff nearly single-handedly obtained the support of the Post Commander to allow our group's involvement in several unofficial class functions culminating with a formal Minority Officers' Ball.

Following graduation from CGSC Griff's closest CGSC classmates were reassigned to installations throughout the world while he headed for a tour in Germany. While on temporary duty there, I had the opportunity to visit and check in with him because I now felt it my duty to stay in touch with him and follow his career and I really enjoyed every opportunity to spend time with him. Once again his sterling reputation as Engineer Battalion Executive Officer and as Commander preceded my visit, for he continued to be widely known as a devoted professional. Our association as comrades in arms culminated in Washington, DC during his assignment as Engineer Branch Chief with the Total Army Personnel Agency and his culminating assignment as Director of Construction and Contracts in the Pentagon. His storied career as a construction engineer, helicopter pilot, instructor, and leader/commander came to a befitting close. During his final military years in DC, our immediate families became extensions of the other so we were terribly disappointed to see the Griffins depart, but knew that our bonds had become lifelong.

Although Griff was offered highly competitive, and highly sought after jobs in the industrial sector in the Washington Metropolitan Area before retiring from the Army, he followed his calling to return home and run his family's business. Like many of his comrades and friends, I fully recognized Griff's desire and commitment to return to his roots, but quietly questioned whether he was a perfect fit for a second career as a mortician not withstanding his father's successes in that avocation. In hindsight, since I intimately knew and understood Griff by then, that thought shouldn't have entered my mind because he's one of the most multi-talented individuals I know. He easily transitioned into life as a civilian and respected businessman in Milledgeville, his hometown, because he always sought new challenges and venues everywhere, whether in another country or at home.

When he advised me of his intent to become a Georgia State Senator, I fully embraced and supported his candidacy from a distance because I was fully aware that he prepared himself for such an office by becoming very politically involved throughout his home state. I was convinced that he was a winner who always achieved his personal and professional goals. When he advised me a few years later that he had become a Democratic candidate for Georgia Lt. Governor, his CGSC classmates and I simply fell in line and supported him during that heavily contested primary race. We regretted that we didn't help him raise the finances to put him over the top. To make amends we gave our unconditional support when he decided to enter into and win his hometown's race for Mayor. Now we simply await his entry into the next phase of his live whether as a politician or businessman. Griff often says that God takes care of us! As a Godly servant, devoted leader of his immediate and extended families, gifted professional, respected statesman in local and state politics, I am extremely proud to call him my trusted confidant and beloved friend.

Preface

Legacy to Legend: Winners Make It Happen reflects one man's quest for knowledge, excellence, and social change. Celebrating an illustrious career as a U.S. Army colonel, war pilot, state senator, mayor, coach, and businessman, Floyd L. Griffin, Jr., exemplifies a man with a determined spirit. The dapper Georgia native with a penchant for cowboy boots and unlit cigars made political history when, in 1994, he became the first African American to be elected to the state Senate from Georgia's 25th District. Griffin's election to the Senate marked the first time since Reconstruction that a black candidate won office in a rural, majority-white legislative district in Georgia. Six years later, he blazed another history-making trail when he became the first black mayor of his hometown of Milledgeville, Georgia.

Griffin's social activism began during the Civil Rights Movement, while as a student at Tuskegee Institute (University) in Alabama. After graduating from Tuskegee as a commissioned officer, Griffin flew helicopters for the U.S. Army during the tumult of the Vietnam War. Following a military career that spanned 23 years and included more history-making firsts as officer and commander of various posts, Griffin retired in 1990 as full colonel, one of the Army's highest ranks.

During his military career, Griffin completed a tour of duty in Germany and held a number of key positions. In addition to being a pilot, he was a flight instructor and commander of a construction-engineer company. He served as a logistics officer, battalion executive officer, and director of engineering and housing. From 1984 to 1986, Griffin commanded an engineering battalion at Fort Stewart, Georgia, under Norman H. Schwartzkopf (Commanding General, 24th Infantry Division), and from 1986 to 1990, he served on the U.S. Army staff at the Pentagon.

Griffin's career also included work as an educator. He was an assistant professor of military science at both Wake Forest University and Winston-Salem State University in North Carolina. While at Winston-Salem, he served as director of ROTC and coached the offensive backfield on two undefeated championship football teams. He was a part-time instructor with the University of Chicago's extension program in Germany and was director of Facilities and Engineering at Milledgeville's Georgia Military College. Later, he served as a part-time instructor at Georgia State College & University in Milledgeville.

As Georgia State Senator, Griffin directed allocations and grants to the counties he represented. He effected land deals and architectural improvements, and worked ardently to create legislation to help the State's dairy farmers preserve their livelihoods. He worked to ensure the financial stability of Georgia's public schools and to guarantee that the General Assembly had a role in any decisions to be made regarding the privatization of state facilities and institutions.

In the Georgia General Assembly, Griffin served as secretary of the Defense and Veterans Affairs Committee. He was chairman of the Interstate Cooperations Committee and was a member of the Senate Study Committee on the Privatization of Governmental Services, the Higher Education Committee, the Influential Rules Committee, and the Health and Human Services Committee.

Griffin earned a Bachelor of Science degree in Building Construction from Tuskegee and a Master's degree in Contract and Procurement Management from the Florida Institute of Technology. He is a graduate of the Army Command and General Staff College, as well as the National War College. He earned an Associate's degree from Gupton-Jones College of Funeral Service. Today, Griffin is funeral director, embalmer, and president of Slater's Funeral Home, owned and operated for decades in Milledgeville by the Griffin family.

Active in the community, Griffin served as Milledgeville's mayor from 2002 to 2006. He was the first African American to become a member of the Rotary Club of Milledgeville. His memberships also include the Warren-Hawkins Post of the American Legion, Milledgeville United Negro College Fund, National War College Alumni Association, Baldwin County NAACP and SCLC, Milledgeville Chamber of Commerce, Prince Hall Free and Accepted Masons, Milledgeville-Baldwin County Film Commission and Milledgeville-Baldwin County Olympic Committee. He served on the boards of Central State Hospital Foundations, Inc.; Milledgeville Evening Optimist Club; Baldwin County Council on Substance Abuse; and Milledgeville-Baldwin County Rape Crisis Center. He is a former member of the board of directors of the Georgia College and State University (GCSU) Intercollegiate Athletic Association and the GCSU Foundation. He was also chairman of the search committee for the establishment of the Milledgeville-Baldwin County Human Relations Commission.

A life member of Omega Psi Phi Fraternity, Griffin has been inducted also into the Sigma Pi Phi Fraternity. He received the Milledgeville-Baldwin County Chamber of Commerce Community Service Award in 1993 and was honored by Gupton-Jones College with its Distinguished Service Award for the advancement of the funeral-service profession. Griffin presently serves on the Board of Directors of the National Center for Missing and Exploited Children, Alexandria, Virginia.

Griffin and his wife, Nathalie Huffman Griffin, are the parents of two sons, Brian and Eric, and have six grandchildren. The Griffins are members of Trinity Christian Methodist Episcopal Church in Milledgeville.

Part I
The Making of an Independent Man

Chapter I

The Making of an Independent Man

For as long as I can remember, my father, Floyd L. Griffin, Sr., worked for himself. This was rare in my father's day, for working-class blacks, more than any other group, comprised the labor pool of farmers, factory workers, domestics and others who worked for white families and white-owned businesses throughout the South. My Daddy, however, was an entrepreneur; an independent business owner serving black families in Middle Georgia counties by delivering the firewood and kindling they needed for heat and cooking.

In such a position, Daddy could have acted with the disdain of one who knows he has a monopoly, but he was not like that. He was a diligent businessman who insisted that his loads be ready to go each day and that each job was delivered on time. He kept good records and even extended credit to people, especially during the winter months, when work for some was slow. For this reason, he developed a loyal customer base and maintained a devoted relationship with the people he served. My brother Toney, my uncle Bennie and I made up my Daddy's team. From us, he tolerated no messing around on the job. Sometimes our horseplay and competitive spirit earned us a whack, because Daddy was serious about his business. Through his service to others, he taught us integrity, honesty, responsibility and loyalty.

Daddy lived all his life in the central Georgia town of Milledgeville. The seat of Baldwin County, Milledgeville served as state capital until that honor was transferred to Atlanta in 1868. The historic district includes the Old State Capitol and Governor's Mansion, as well as a number of noteworthy private homes.

In the early 1950's, racial segregation in public schools was the norm across America despite the 1954 *Brown v. Board of Education* Supreme Court decision. Milledgeville was no exception. Although schools in a given district were supposed to be equal, the allocation and accommodations for black schools were significantly less than those of their white counterparts. Baldwin County had some seven black schools and thirty black churches charged with the responsibility of teaching the coming generations, of which I was a part. Despite being materially poor, Milledgeville's black community was wealthy in character, hope and principle. The teachers, parents, and others in the community worked together to ensure that the children succeeded educationally. Many of the simple truths and solid principles I inherited from honest, hard-working and loving parents, and from teachers and other community members, fueled my quest for excellence, growth and achievement. I am convinced that their efforts contributed to my becoming, years later, the first person of color elected as state senator representing Georgia's 25th District, which includes Baldwin County. I also became the first black mayor of Milledgeville, a city that to this day still has a majority-white population.

Milledgeville today is a quaint city of lovely tree-lined streets, antebellum structures, peaceful parks and a modest business district. It boasts an elite college community, and with a hovering tranquility and pockets of rustic communities, it is never far from its rural past. The city is also a fisherman's paradise. With 15,330 acres of water and 417 miles of shoreline, Lake Sinclair is an important recreational resource for all of Baldwin County. The state government has a strong presence in the county, with Middle Georgia Correctional Institution,

Central State Hospital, Youth Development Center, Georgia War Veterans Home, and three colleges—Georgia State College & University, Georgia Military College, and Middle Georgia Technical College.

My family's presence in Milledgeville began when my paternal grandfather, Willie T. Griffin, moved his family there in the 1920s. He was born in Wilkinson County, Georgia, and became an AME minister who lived to be 100 years old. The woman he married, Eva, was a lovely lady with strikingly beautiful features. I was about five years old when my grandfather died and about fourteen when my grandmother Eva died. My grandparents never failed to show pride in their son, my father, and love for their grandchildren.

My Daddy served in the U.S. Army as a military policeman during World War II. His military photograph, which adorned the mantel of our combination family and dining room, was a reminder of the days when he proudly served his country. Military veterans were afforded unique benefits, such as the G.I. Bill and educational opportunities many other blacks did not have. My Daddy often spoke of places he had visited while in the military, places I would read about in books. Those experiences gave him the desire to want more out of life than American society usually offered blacks. Mind you, in the 1940s in rural South, it was a courageous effort for a black man to embrace the goal of becoming a businessman instead of taking his so-called rightful place as a laborer for someone else.

My mother, Ruth Evans Griffin, was, in my opinion, a Milledgeville peach. She became the principle reason my Daddy found his way to church every Sunday. When they were courting, Daddy had to be on his best behavior and perform decently in school, because Mother's parents would not allow her to associate with a young man that didn't have his life together. Their relationship blossomed over the years, and my Daddy promised her parents that he would always give her the love and favor she deserved and that they expected. Mother finished high school and married Daddy, then worked for a number of years as a beautician before devoting herself full time to the other family businesses. Her parents were Johnnie and Hattie Taylor Evans. I have a child's recollection of Hattie's mother, my great-grandmother Mamie Taylor. What stands out most in my memory of her is that she was part Native American and a very pretty lady.

As a young man still in school, my father developed an entrepreneurial spirit while working as a landscaper and handyman for white families. He was a positive, energetic person who not only played on his school's football and basketball teams, but as a teenager made as much money as many adults. He was resourceful and an independent thinker. His routine was to carry landscaping tools with him to a client's house on his way to school each day. This allowed him to have his tools already in place when he returned to do the work. He supported his family economically, improving their lot and supporting his siblings' education. In those days, it was customary in black families for employed members to help support those who attended school, especially college.

Before finishing high school, Daddy was drafted into the Army during World War II. After his discharge, he worked at Central State Hospital as a painter before starting his firewood business. He could have forgotten about formal education at that point, becoming consumed, instead, by the responsibility of caring for a family. But Daddy did not do that. He attended a veterans' night-school program and earned his high-school diploma. It impressed the family that he took this step, but it did not surprise us, for my father was a good teacher and a great example of manhood and parenthood. At a time when most blacks were under the daily bequest of whites, my father's independence was evident in the fact that his interaction with whites was largely limited to the trips he made to the sawmill. There, he bought slabs, the back portion of the tree that is cut to make firewood. Daddy was also a spiritual man. Not only did he serve as a deacon at Union Baptist Church, the home church of our family for many years, he also believed that serving others and building relationships yielded faithful results. He used his wood business to reinforce these beliefs in the community.

Like my father, my mother did not believe in working for others. She and Daddy opened a grocery store, which became a thriving business, and Mother enrolled in beauty school. After she graduated, the store was expanded to create a beauty shop. Mother continued to work exclusively in the shop until they decided to open a dry-cleaning business. Especially in the later years, she worked in the store and dry cleaners, and retired several years ago from the family funeral home.

Although my mother's family attended Second Macedonia Baptist Church, Mother joined Union Baptist after she married Daddy. Today, she serves as mother of the church. She and Daddy were married 62 years before his death. In my opinion, they are a magnificent model of a strong marital union. Daddy made sure Mother was accustomed to being treated like a queen, somebody special, and to us, she certainly is. She was spoiled during his lifetime and is still being spoiled, to a degree, something I know would please my father, for she was his heart.

Bennie Evans, my mother's youngest brother that my parents raised along with us, is retired and assists in the family business on a part-time basis.

My younger brother, Toney W. Griffin, now lives in Atlanta. He attended Morehouse College. He recently retired from Delta Airlines and is currently working in real estate, something he has enjoyed doing over the years. He has two adult children, a son and daughter. Toney had some interesting recollections of growing up in the Griffin family.

"As the second son, my Daddy named me Toney, a different spelling of the name than usual. It came from to him from a friendship that he had with a little French boy who use to hang around near the base where he was stationed while in the Army

during World War II. The kid was fascinated by Americans and particularly Black Americans as my Daddy was probably one of the first he had ever met. Toney apparently had a great little personality and longed to hear stories about America. Everyone embraced this kid's innocence in the midst of his country being torn apart by war. So my Daddy named me after his little friend who he knew he'd never see again, but whose genuineness and quest for life he would never forget."

"Daddy and Mother were set in their ways as it relates to using the name given to you. They visited me once in Atlanta, where I thought I'd show them one of my real estate signs, as I sold and invested in real estate in addition to working for Delta Airlines. Upon seeing the sign, Daddy said, "Where is your middle name? We named you Toney Willis Griffin. Why don't you have all of your name on this sign?" That's something only a parent would say."

"My Daddy was the hardest working man I have ever known. It seemed he was always preparing for something, finishing something or fixing something. After the military he worked as a painter at the hospital for some years before transferring his interest into building a wood business. He always worked for himself. Growing up, Floyd, my uncle Bennie and myself made up his work team. I was the youngest and the smallest yet very little mercy was exhibited as I had to carry my load. Naturally, we kept a level of joking, games and small talk going but Daddy didn't tolerate us playing around too much. There were times when he had to straighten us all out. That was something I never looked forward to because it appeared that I got the same degree of whipping that the older, bigger guys received. For the most part, Daddy imparted simple principles of business and integrity that we all adopted."

"Our product in the firewood business was the primary source for cooking and heating homes throughout the region. Daddy stressed the importance of serving the people who made his business possible even in times when they could not afford to pay us. There were many people who worked seasonally and who struggled under the pressure of unemployment, racism and limited access."

"When we came home from school each day there was a note left for us on the window of the truck with specific instructions of what Daddy wanted us to do after we finished our homework."

"I applied and was accepted to attend Morehouse College in 1964. At Morehouse I had the opportunity to be inspired by the legendary Dr. Benjamin E. Mays and a student body of supremely talented young Black men who were destined to be leaders in business and industry. Michael Lomax. President of UNCF was one of my classmates. Socially we were right in the middle of three campuses of women at Spelman, Clark College and Morris Brown plus a nursing school at Grady Hospital. Some friends and I lucked up on an opportunity to live rent-free in one of the most popular apartment complexes near school. So we became lifeguards and management help which was a dream job at Normandy Forest Apartments. Having that apartment and a pool too, took my stock to another level but that was pleasantly short-lived. This was also the place that I met Barbara, the woman who would become my wife. She and her family had an apartment downstairs from us. So as it turns out, Floyd wasn't the only one to go to college and find a wife. We have been happily married for 41 years. We have a son, Toney Wyndero and a daughter, Tonesha Dawn."

"Floyd was at Tuskegee and was a drum major leading the marching band at the football games. Morehouse has a near perfect record of losses to Tuskegee who's football team was a powerhouse. Our teams met each year for a classic game in Columbus. That's where I had a chance to see him in action and get together with him after the game. Floyd also worked in the student activist movement and worked in Alabama one or two of the summers. He had also met Nathalie who was from Birmingham, so in time, he was making trips to her hometown more frequently than going back to Milledgeville. We would get together in Atlanta sometimes and he even lived with me there for a short while after graduation. He took a position with an engineering company while his military orders were being processed."

"Over the years, we've kept in touch and have made major family outings out of traveling to Floyd's graduations and pinning ceremonies. The Griffin family has been present at many of his appointments, including when he made full colonel. Floyd took me on tours of places like the National War College and The Pentagon in Washington, D.C., in areas that only high ranking officers were allowed to go. Like a typical big brother, Floyd has always been one who could make things happen."

My sister, Delbra A. Griffin Waller, is a graduate of Paine College in Augusta, Georgia. She has an adult son and a granddaughter and resides in Milledgeville, where she serves as vice president and funeral director at Slater's Funeral Home. She also had some things to say about growing up in the Griffin family.

"I am the youngest of my brother's siblings. I grew up thinking Floyd and Toney were the best brothers a sister could have. My family always made each of us feel special. As the only girl, I marveled in the loving care of a God fearing and wonderful mother and father, absolutely great aunts, uncles, cousins, and four wise and adoring grandparents. The joy of my small town existence was the loving support of the entire Griffin, Evans, Taylor and Jackson families."

"Our Daddy, Floyd, Sr., met and married his life partner, the former Ruth Evans, our mother, and carried on a union that lasted 62 years. Their life together was an example to families who either lived in the same town or the next town over all of their years together. I grew up in a God-fearing, proud, determined, hard working, entrepreneurial family. Our Daddy was in the wood business providing fire wood for cooking and heating homes. Floyd, Toney and Uncle Benny made up Daddy's main team, which was in addition to his other employees. Daddy stressed life principles each day to his crew. These were the simple truths of life that he lived by and was known by. He was first a man of God, and a man of his word. He was a fair, giving man who was a living example of the values he stressed to his team. He challenged them to show initiative, be self reliant and be dependable. His customers gave him an opportunity to be successful in his business. He kept good records and extended credit to everyone who needed it."

"Daddy was the son of a country preacher. Papa Griffin was an independent thinker and a businessman. He sold fire coal and he hauled it on a horse drawn wagon. On Sunday afternoons and whenever he had an opportunity, he expressed his displeasure with the conditions of segregation. He was quite radical for this time, almost to the point that people feared his messages and conversations might get back to the people who supported segregation. Daddy sort of inherited some of his personality honestly. Papa was his own man, but he also served the people. Our Daddy in his own business endeavors was a servant of the people. Daddy had this take charge boldness about him, but yet he was a very humble man. Floyd and Toney both inherited this quality quite honestly. Our mother owned and operated a very successful beauty

salon. She was a cosmetologist who hired two other operators. Both parents were a team and whatever they pursued, they worked together to complete it. They both were independent thinkers in their own right. They also owned a dry cleaning business, rental properties, a grocery store and the funeral home in which the family owns and manages today."

"Watching both parents......they helped me to set goals and dream big. I am blessed to have had over-achievers as parents. I am blessed that my relationship with our mother is still evolving and maturing as she remains the true joy of our lives."

"As we began to make decisions about college, Mother and Daddy directed us to HBCUs. Floyd chose Tuskegee Institute in Alabama because they offered Engineering as a major and the ROTC program that would pay most of his college tuition and make him an officer in the military. Toney elected to attend Morehouse College in Atlanta, the college made famous by Dr. Martin Luther king, Jr., Maynard Jackson and many others. I decided to attend Paine College in Augusta, GA, another great college. Floyd went away to school and brought back with him "my sister", the woman who would become his wife, Nathalie. I can never thank him enough for bringing to us such a beautiful, peaceful and loving person as Nathalie into our family. She is truly the sister that I never had. Furthermore, she has the qualities that my mother has which I'm sure affected his decision, and he apparently has the qualities and persona that became the perfect match that has lasted for 42 years. I am blessed to have the family that I have."

Chapter 2

Childhood in Middle Georgia

Growing up in Milledgeville, my life consisted of going to school each weekday, engaging in sports and other extracurricular activities, and helping Daddy in business. Each Sunday, our family would go to church and visit our grandparents and neighbors. Mother always prepared something special for that day, like her legendary fried chicken, or my favorite, turkey and dressing. During the week, Daddy required that we all pitch in regularly with his businesses. We each had assignments and were expected to fit work into our schedules. My brother Toney, my uncle Bennie and I worked with him as part of the team in all his ventures. My sister, Delbra, helped around the house and in the store where we sold grocery items, cigarettes, cold drinks, and a few supplies. For a time, our store and home was one of the few places in the area with a telephone, which made it a popular meeting place. We served black and white clientele, working-class people like ourselves.

Daddy was a strict, old-fashioned disciplinarian, as were many black parents of that time. This helped create a strong sense of community and a respect for people. Children especially had to respect adults, and parents gave other adults the authority to straighten you out if you, as a child, got out of hand. And when word got back to your parents—you got it again. This was, of course, done out of love and with a desire to make sure we developed the qualities we needed to become responsible and successful adults. To that end, my parents always provided well for us; we were never without the basic needs. In fact, few people I knew at the time went hungry, because the community was there for its members. We always shared with our neighbors—a cup of sugar or anything else they needed. Our church had an annual homecoming during which members would come back to fellowship and celebrate the church's anniversary. Everyone would gather together and enjoy delicious foods laid out picnic-style. Some brought boxes of food, others even barbecued hogs, as the event was always a giant reunion and feast.

But the community wasn't always a pleasant sight. The conditions under which many of our people lived—the shotgun houses, etc.—were at times distressing to my family and me. It became my Daddy's commitment to demonstrate the biblical principle, "To whom much is given, much is expected." Therefore, he always extended courtesy to the less fortunate families on his wood-delivery route. He would go by on Saturday evenings or Sunday mornings and collect whatever money his customers could afford to pay to settle their accounts. In the wintertime, regardless of whether they could pay or not, Daddy made sure his customers had a supply of wood. To many of his store clients, he extended credit. In response, people would come in on payday and, in most cases, would pay up. Daddy kept a ledger as a record of accounts, though he never pressed people who could not afford to pay him. His ledger gradually became a family record of births, graduations, marriages, and deaths in the community, as well as his record of major purchases.

Thanks to my parents' example, I never doubted my dreams for the future. When later I decided I wanted to become an Army officer and a construction professional, I fully believed I was capable of doing so. I was courageous enough to play football with the big boys even though I only weighed 110 pounds, soaking wet, in high school.

My confidence existed not only because of my parents' example, but because of teachers who challenged me to excel in my coursework and activities. Back then, a teacher was as respected in the community as a doctor, though they certainly were not paid as much. Our teachers were dedicated to empowering members of the next generation to take their rightful place in what the teachers hoped would be a changing world. Because of these wonderful people and my parents' example, I always felt that I could make things happen. My sister, brother, uncle and I were blessed to have my parents and I hope our lives have turned out to bring honor to Ruth Evans Griffin and Floyd L. Griffin, Sr.

School Days

I attended Mount Hill Church School until third grade. One of my favorite teachers was Mrs. Christine Ray, a proper and dedicated educator who shared books with me that started my formal learning process. In the fourth grade, I entered Carver Elementary and High School, one of the traditional all–black schools, and remained there until seventh grade. My brother, Toney, sister Delbra, Uncle Bennie and I attended there until J.F. Boddie High School was built. We attended Boddie, which was named after one of the first black medical doctors from Milledgeville. Later, Boddie became a middle school. Today, it is Baldwin High School.

One of my favorite teachers, Mrs. Rosa Lofton, had a significant impact on my growth. Her wise counsel and personal concern helped her students to embrace her teachings and prepared us for life. As a premier English teacher, Mrs. Rosa Lofton demanded that we speak and write well. She taught with an impassioned knowledge of the language, and she introduced us to the joy of reading and to a host of accomplished black writers. She also taught us etiquette—even how to eat soup!— (always dip away from you) and other things that helped prepare us for life.

Another impressive school official was Professor Joseph M. Graham, principal of Boddie High School and a family friend. Professor Graham worked tirelessly to make sure any student who wanted to go to college was prepared for that step. His brother was a vice president at Paine College in Augusta, and as a result, many Boddie students went to Paine. Professor Graham and his staff made sure we understood the need to finish high school. He stressed the importance of education and the positive impact it would have on the future of our families.

In addition to the teachers' encouragement, I experienced growth from other avenues, as well. Becoming involved with activities such as the yearbook committee, the band, and the choir helped to develop my confidence and speaking ability. I also played football for several years. I had the distinction of being the smallest member on the team, but I had a lot of heart—and speed! Although there was some concern about my size, I was able to play and never missed a practice. During those times, the member of a team had to fulfill several roles. I was a running back, a line backer and a bit of a quarterback. I also played clarinet in the high-school band and later was a drum major. When I entered Tuskegee Institute a few years later, I did the same thing—played clarinet for a couple of years, which led to my becoming the head drum major.

Professor Graham significantly impacted my decision to enter Tuskegee. As I have said, he was committed to seeing that everyone who desired to attend college had the opportunity to do so, and for this reason, he stressed the importance of earning a high-school diploma. African American youths, he believed, should achieve a high standard. Many of my schoolmates did just that.

Clark D. Lucky – classmate and friend

"**Floyd Griffin** *is my friend. I think we met in the 6th or 7th grade and we finished High School together. We were about the same height until our junior year. I can remember returning to school from our summer break; Floyd had grown at least* *six or seven inches. He was six feet and I was stuck at five feet six."*

"Floyd was an average student in school. However, he worked diligently. He was always interested in learning as much as he could about the subjects we were taking."

"His father had a lumber yard and some days Floyd would work before he came to school. He was always a hard worker. I can remember that all of the boys in our home room class were called to the principal's office one day. We were guilty of a prank and the principal decided that we needed a swat for this prank. We were all given two swats and when Floyd received his swats, saw dust came from his pants. We all thought this was very funny. From this incident, He was given the nickname "Griff" and later he was referred to as "Gripp".

"After we finished High School, we went our separate ways. Floyd attended Tuskegee and I attended Savannah State. We would only see each other in the summer. When we finished college we drifted apart. We may have seen each other three times in a span of thirty years. However, our friendship remained the same. When we see each other we talk about what is happening in our lives".

"We are very proud of Floyd Griffin, Jr.'s accomplishments and achievements. I am proud to have him as a friend."

Allen Nelson was the Assistant Football Coach at Boddie High School when Floyd Griffin decided he wanted to play football. *"When Floyd went out for football, he wasn't one of the heavier guys,"* said Nelson. *"In fact, he was pretty small. But he had a lot of heart and he took a lot of hits and continued to come back."*

Griffin also walked about 4 miles home each day. *"That really impressed me,"* Nelson continued. *"He put that kind of determination into everything he did. He had a strong desire to be a player and he worked hard toward that end. He seldom played, but he stayed on the team because of his determination. Floyd was persistent and when he wanted something, he would not give up."*

"I was heading up the 4-H when Floyd was in high school," said Outley Faulk, another close friend. *"He was much more dedicated than the average young person. A lot of those kids would sign up for 4-H just to get out of regular*

classes, but Floyd dedicated his all. Even today, I can still say that Floyd is a very sincere, dedicated person. He puts his heart and soul into anything he does and he does it right. He is a wonderful role model for young men."

Willetta Stanley has known Griffin practically all of her life and is ready to share good memories about him.

"I first met Floyd in the eighth grade, and we were friends from the ninth to the twelfth grade at J.F. Boddie High School. He was always very ambitious in school."

Stanley's relationship with Griffin resumed years after they had left school.

"I remember our 1976 class reunion. Floyd came back from Washington and we got reacquainted. Anytime he would come home, he would come by and see me.

"I always did the catering for Floyd anytime he had a reception for something. He would call me up and say, 'Willetta, I want you to do all the food.' I was always glad to help him in any way I could. In fact, I am a seamstress and I did a lot of alterations and hemming of his pants for him; he always wanted to look nice. I also volunteered daily at his campaign headquarters when he ran for the Senate. I made phone calls, addressed envelopes—anything he needed."

Stanley says Griffin has always exhibited kindness and generosity. *"I remember awhile back when my job closed and I was down on my luck. He came by my house several times and would squeeze my hand and he always left money in it. He was just like that. Years ago, one of our classmates' house burned and Floyd donated money to help the family.*

ABOUT HIS PROFESSIONALISM, SHE SAYS:

"Floyd is a very precise man, very punctual. Time is very important to him. I like that about Floyd; if he says he's going to do something, he does it. Floyd has really encouraged me throughout the years to strive to achieve a lot in life, like he's done. He has helped me at some of the lowest points in my life. When he called me and said he wanted me to be in his book, it was one of the greatest honors of my life."

THE RATTLERS

Captain: James Lunsford
Co-Captain: George Hogan

Coaches: Charles Williams
Allen C. Nelson, Robert Cooper

SENIORS

FIRST ROW, L-R.: Elijah Freeman, Eugene Culver, Eugene Abrams, James Lunsford. SECOND ROW: Joseph Calhoun, Robert Hartry, Emory Austin, Floyd Griffin, Josh Milner.

JIM CROW DAYS AND MILLEDGEVILLE

In the Milledgeville of my childhood, adults in the black community were positive role models and ordinary proud folks who never viewed themselves as inferior human beings. Even though racial discrimination and Jim Crow laws were common in the South, society didn't have the vast news sources of today are able to expose every major act of racist violence that goes on in the world the moment it occurs. Therefore, blacks who were isolated from much of the active hatred of the day—the church burnings, beatings and lynchings—could almost believe we were better off, as a people, than we actually were. That was the case with us in Milledgeville, which accounted for our failure to feel "low class" in connection with our white neighbors. But every once in a while, something happened that reminded us that others did not feel as good about us as we did about ourselves.

I remember an incident that happened when I was in middle school. A young white kid came into our store and ordered a soda. He said something to me that was inappropriate—right there in my parents' store. He was trying to pull a "white power" move on me. Seeing that I was angered and not backing down, he threw the soda on me and dashed out the door. I chased him. He jumped across a ditch and I caught him and laid it on him a little bit. He went back and told his father, who came and spoke with him. Daddy didn't back down; he didn't play that black-and-white submission game. My Daddy told the boy's father that he didn't want his son coming to our store anymore and that if he came around in a disrespectful manner again, he was going to get his butt whipped again. When I think back, I realize the danger that my Daddy—and I could have encountered because of this incident.

Milledgeville, as did many Southern towns and cities, had a peculiar quality. Despite deep-seated racist beliefs, there were communities in which blacks and whites lived virtually next door to one another. My family lived in an area where whites were only a few blocks away. This did not, however, erase the lines of social segregation. We Milledgeville blacks might have felt innately equal to our white neighbors, but we knew our "place" in their social structure, and they had the power to enforce their belief that we were second-class citizens. There were establishments like McCoy's Café, which served blacks through a special entrance on the side of the building, and only for carry-out orders. Seating was for white patrons only, and the two sides of the store were divided by a counter. There were drugstores where blacks could order but could not sit at the lunch counter to enjoy their refreshments. Schools were segregated; black students were issued old hand-me-down books, and because of a lack of facilities, some schools were conducted in churches.

Fortunately, in 1957, there was a massive improvement in Milledgeville's school facilities. The state and county, in an attempt to comply with the federal mandates following the 1954 *Brown vs. Board of Education* decision, joined forces with several progressive whites to make educational improvements in Baldwin County. A number of new schools for black students were built during that period, enabling us to retire some of our older facilities. The new schools and additional teachers made a significant difference in the learning environment.

I remember the excitement I felt going to the new high school in the seventh grade. I was thirteen years old at the time. But as excited as we were about having shiny new desks and walls and floors, our teachers never let us forget that what was most important was learning and achieving success. Their admonition paid off. The proud black graduates who left our little town returned home as doctors, lawyers, retired military personnel, and other professionals of note. They found themselves able to compete with the best and brightest from the white community, those who had always had the advantages we had been denied. I often wonder how we were able to accomplish so much during that segregated era.

Touchstones and other Memories: Military Aspirations

The earliest memory I have of seeing a man in uniform came from my Daddy's smiling picture on the mantle at home, the photo he took during his military service days in World War II. I don't recall ever seeing my Daddy in uniform in person, because I was too young. However, it did impress me to see other black men in our community who would return home in uniform, looking sharp and having what I perceived to be a new outlook on life. I decided that one day I, too, would join the U.S. Army.

My parents hired a contractor to build a store next to our home. The man impressed me with his sense of organization and talents as planner, carpenter, cement worker, and bricklayer. I liked the precision he used to bring corners of walls and other planes together. The contractor orchestrated the entire process, using my Daddy and his team as helpers. I was so fascinated by the experience that I wanted to be a bricklayer. Later, my aspirations broadened; I not only became a bricklayer, I also received a degree in construction engineering from Tuskegee Institute.

I wanted to go into the Army as well as enter the construction field, but there weren't many black colleges that offered both programs. Tuskegee did. In fact, its ROTC program was famous for the huge numbers of high-ranking black officers who got their start in it. Two of these were black generals, Chappie James and Benjamin Davis, men I knew about and respected. Another reason I found the school appealing was because I learned that with Uncle Sam's help, I could have a considerable amount of my college tuition paid for while pursuing a commission and a degree in my specialty. So I turned my Georgia feet in the direction of Alabama to step into the strange new world of Tuskegee.

Chapter 3

Tuskegee Institute: A New Beginning

The birth of my alma mater, Tuskegee University, was the result of a political bargain conceived by a black man—not Booker T. Washington, the school's famous founding president, but a former slave named Lewis Adams. A nineteenth-century black-community leader in the town of Tuskegee, Adams could read and write, and he worked as a tinsmith, shoemaker, and harness maker. When W.F. Foster, a white candidate seeking reelection to the Alabama Senate, approached Adams to ask how Foster could gain the support of African Americans in Macon County, Adams struck a deal on behalf of his people. In exchange for securing the black vote for Foster, Adams told the senator he wanted a school for blacks. Foster carried out his promise, and with the assistance of Arthur L. Brooks, a colleague in the House of Representatives, House Bill 165 was passed for the establishment of a "Negro Normal School in Tuskegee."

The legislation authorized the state to appropriate $2,000 to the school for teachers' salaries. Adams, Thomas Dryer, and M. B. Swanson formed the board of commissioners that organized the school. They had no land, buildings, or teachers—only state legislation authorizing the project. George W. Campbell, a former slave owner, replaced Dryer as commissioner, and it was Campbell, through his nephew, who sent word to Hampton Institute in Virginia, looking for a black teacher.

Booker T. Washington, a former slave who had become an educated man, answered the call. Consequently, on July 4, 1881, Tuskegee Institute began operations in a one-room shanty located near Butler Chapel African Methodist Episcopal Zion Church. Thirty adults represented the first class, and Washington was principal and first teacher. Not long afterward, he moved the campus to a 100-acre abandoned plantation, which became the nucleus of the present site.

Washington was a highly skilled organizer and fund-raiser who based his school's mission on the philosophy that vocational education, taught with care and fostered into excellence, was the key to blacks' success. He illustrated this point by creating a tough curriculum that required students to attend classes while working as laborers for the school. In fact, the early classes of Tuskegee students constructed their own campus buildings! Under Washington's leadership, Tuskegee rose to national prominence. In 1892, again through legislation, Tuskegee Normal and Industrial Institute was granted authority to act independent of the state of Alabama. After learning about the many achievements of Booker T. Washington and those of Tuskegee researcher Dr. George Washington Carver, my decision to attend Tuskegee an easy one.

Booker Washington served as principal from 1881 until his death in 1915, at age 59. A series of effective presidents succeeded him. Under Robert R. Moton, who served from 1915 until 1935, the institute donated land to the federal government to construct the Tuskegee Veteran's Administration Hospital. Opened in 1923, it became the first such hospital staffed by black professionals and, like the institute, became a status symbol for those blacks who worked there.

Dr. Frederick D. Patterson, Moton's successor, oversaw the establishment of the School of Veterinary Medicine at Tuskegee, which for generations produced most of the country's black veterinarians.

He is credited with founding in 1945 the United Negro College Fund, which to date has raised more than $1 billion for student aid. Dr. Patterson also brought the Tuskegee Airmen flight-training program to the institute. The all-black squadrons were decorated World War II combat veterans whose unique and powerful presence influenced thousands of blacks to join the military—and the Airmen were a factor in my decision to attend Tuskegee. I strongly believe that along with heavyweight boxing champ Joe Louis' knockout of Max Smelling, the Tuskegee Airmen's achievements set the stage for America to win World War II.

When I became a student at Tuskegee, Dr. Luther H. Foster had been president for nine years—since 1953. It was on his watch that the Civil Rights Movement transformed the campus and the surrounding city into a hotbed of student activism, racial tensions, and legal battles. When Foster left two decades later, Dr. Benjamin F. Payton began his tenure, in 1981. Under Payton's leadership, campus construction flourished. The Tuskegee University National Center for Bioethics in Research and Health Care, as well as the Tuskegee Airmen National Historic Site, were launched. The General Daniel "Chappie" James Center for Aerospace Science and Health Education was constructed—the largest athletic arena in the Southern Intercollegiate Athletic Conference (SIAC). Also, the Kellogg Conference Center, one of twelve worldwide, was completed as a renovation and expansion of historic Dorothy Hall.

In 1985, Tuskegee Institute became Tuskegee University and has since begun offering doctoral programs in integrative biosciences, and materials science and engineering. The College of Business and Information Sciences was established and professionally accredited, and the College of Engineering, Architecture and Physical Sciences was expanded to include the only aerospace engineering department at an HBCU (historically black college and university).

At the time of Booker T. Washington's death, there were one

thousand five hundred students at Tuskegee, a two-million-dollar endowment, forty trades (we call them *majors* today), one hundred fully equipped buildings, and some two hundred faculty members. Today, the university boasts more than three thousand students on a campus that, with farm and forest land, includes some five thousand acres and more than seventy buildings—a far cry from the one-room shanty thirty adult students filled back in 1881.

Entering Tuskegee symbolized a new direction and a new life for me. I enrolled in the fall of 1962 as a young, bright-eyed country boy, drawn to the school by an ROTC program that paid a large portion of my tuition and opened the way for me to obtain a construction-engineering degree. I graduated in 1967 with a Bachelor of Science degree in Building Construction and a commission as a second lieutenant in the U.S. Army Corps of Engineers. During the five years I spent at Tuskegee, I did a huge amount of growing up in a short period of time, especially during my first year. Tuskegee was an oasis of young, brilliant, aggressive and beautiful black people. I was amazed to be in the company of so many young students and professors who had come from all parts of the country. The fast pace of college life and the pressures school administrators placed on freshmen to maintain good work and study habits was overwhelming, at times, but thanks to the excellent educators who had taught me in Milledgeville, I was ready for the challenge.

Someone who also benefited from Tuskegee's instructors as much as I did was Gwen Patton, a true friend and one of the leaders of the student movement. Gwen earned bachelor's degrees in English and history from Tuskegee, where she also served as student-body president. It was while she was a scholar activist at Tuskegee that state officials told her she would never get a job in Alabama because of her freedom activities. Gwen left the state in 1966 and continued to be involved in activities designed to bring equality and freedom to African Americans. She earned a master's degree from Antioch University

(NY) and at the time of this writing is a Ph.D. candidate with the Union Graduate School. The Interdenominational Institute of Theology (Atlanta, GA) conferred upon her an honorary doctorate.

"I was student-body president at the time that Floyd and I matriculated at Tuskegee Institute," said Patton. "There were just hundreds of students who desired to be change-agents, involved in making a difference. I remember Floyd as being part of the ROTC. The ROTC students who were cadets were very supportive of the student movement and the Civil Rights Movement, in general. Floyd Griffin was one of the leaders in that contingent, along with myself, Eldridge Burns and McKinley Harris. They, as black Americans, had reservations about what was going on in Viet Nam. And of course we were very, very concerned about what we called "selective position" as it related to their status within the ROTC. But they saw themselves as leaders within the ROTC and with the "white slave" question; they didn't see their involvement in the military as a contradiction. Of course, I was never opposed to the ROTC within the black perspective because many of our students had a need for that program because it was also a financial-support means for them to complete their studies and get their degrees. So, we never saw that as a contradiction—being in the student movement, opposing the war in Viet Nam, and being in the ROTC simultaneously."

"Floyd went on and made progressive and positive changes within the military, particularly as it relates to being representative of those blacks who came out of our experience with the desire to excel."

Dr. Patton has served as educational administrator for Pride, Inc., in Washington, D.C.; head of Communications Skills Instruction for the School of Contemporary Studies, Brooklyn College, City University of New York; visiting lecturer at Goddard College in Plainfield, Vermont, and Seaton Hall University in New Jersey; academic advisor head at Alabama State University; and Capital Campaign Coordinator for Tuskegee University.

My first year of higher learning introduced me to another type of education—reality. The campus and city of Tuskegee was truly a college community. Everything centered on the pursuit of education, and most of the people with whom we had contact were professors and other educated staff who lived in relative material comfort. However, just a few miles outside the city were some of the most impoverished areas in the state. I had never seen that degree of difference in the living conditions among black people in Georgia. But just beyond the "oasis" of Tuskegee, and throughout Alabama, a virtual armpit of racial oppression trapped the poor and black citizens of the surrounding counties. Many lived in crippling poverty, and most did not have access to critical life-sustaining assistance—an embarrassment in a country that claimed to be the home of the free and the brave.

In response to this disparity—especially after the attention the Civil Rights Movement received from the broadcast struggles in Birmingham, Montgomery, Little Rock and other places—the federal government and well-meaning white outreach organizations searched for solutions to Alabama's national embarrassment. But black college students had their own solution—a sociopolitical movement that found ways to make a difference in the lives of local residents who were suffering at the hands of uncaring officials and racist neighbors. These students waged support efforts to provide meaningful assistance to blacks in the fourteen counties surrounding Tuskegee, and I immediately joined them in this effort. Tuskegee students mobilized, along with groups like the Student Nonviolent Coordinating Committee (SNCC), to provide resources and support to communities in rural Alabama and other Southern states. We helped provide literacy assistance, and voter education and registration. Participating in such meaningful missions, especially under the stress of potentially life-threatening circumstances, made us all grow up in a hurry.

I became aware of the Civil Rights Movement while still a boy in Milledgeville. Even though the national media did not broadcast many of the racial acts of violence that affected our people, we weren't completely in the dark about major events. For instance, through word of mouth, and even by newspaper and TV, we learned about the 1955 Montgomery Bus Boycott and felt victorious when the 352-day protest was a success. I remember the Little Rock Nine school-desegregation incident of 1957; I was thirteen and saw it on TV. Though the black community in my hometown feared for the Arkansas students' safety, we knew in our hearts that they were doing what was right. Their courageous efforts had a great impact on me. I realized that social conditions were going to be changing. I just had no idea, at the time, that I would enter Tuskegee a few years later and have a part in making those changes a reality.

Alabama in 1962 was the cradle of resistance for the Civil Rights Movement, from the boycott in Montgomery to the voting-rights protests in Birmingham and Selma. But other states were settings of resistance, as well. Throughout the South, black college students, in solidarity with what we were doing in Alabama, voiced their concerns for equal rights and opportunity at lunch counters and businesses. Busloads of students traveled to join us in marches in the Montgomery, Selma and Tuskegee areas. Representatives from SNCC and CORE (Congress of Racial Equality) lent support to the Tuskegee movement.

I imagine that anyone who was old enough to understand world events on November 22, 1963 will always remember where they were that day, for that was when President John F. Kennedy was assassinated. I had just left math class when I heard the news, and it was as if the world stopped. People, even grown men, were crying in the streets. Parents were calling their children home from school. Every business and government office closed, and even classes were dismissed. Everyone gathered around the few television sets that were available to watch the unfolding events in disbelief. It was the one incident that truly made us realize how vulnerable we were as a nation. Yet, would you believe that in the good ole' South, there were some that felt that Kennedy got what he deserved? These were the kind of callous people we faced as student protestors.

TICEP (Tuskegee Institute Community Education Program) was founded by Dr. P.B. Phillips, an energetic dean not much older than the students and this organization provided much-needed assistance to poverty-stricken areas in the fourteen counties surrounding Tuskegee. Through Phillips' program, students from across the South got involved in tutoring and efforts to provide health-care assistance and construction-related jobs that enabled blacks to improve the quality of life within their communities.

During the summer of 1964, a large contingent of white students came down from Northern universities to work with TICEP. They were assigned to areas in the Black Belt, such as Selma and Lowndes County, working along with black students, empowering and supporting the people of the poverty-stricken areas. Those of us who assisted these white students found the experience rewarding, though awkward, at times, for we angered Southern whites and blacks who did not want the change we represented or were simply uncomfortable with seeing interracial alliances. On top of that, our task itself was hard. We went into communities where people were not educated, so the activists had to learn how to communicate with those people—how to explain why we were there and exactly what we were trying to accomplish. Change did not come overnight, and the distrust and anger our presence evoked made it an enormously risky activity.

Still, Dean Phillips' summer program experienced successful results, so we continued part of the program into the school year. It became one of the most impressive outreach actions of the time. We saw evidence of its success in the expressions on the faces of people who received our care. I felt blessed by the opportunity to do such purposeful work.

College Days at Tuskegee and TICEP College Outreach Program

DR. PHILLIPS, AS FOUNDER OF TICEP, CAN BEST DESCRIBE THE PROGRAM AND THE SUCCESS WE ENJOYED.

"Floyd Griffin was a tremendous help to me and the TICEP program; he was a good student and a good friend. I relied on Floyd to help carry out many aspects of the Tuskegee Institute Summer Education Program; once extended, it became the Tuskegee Institute Community Education Program. In addition to this, Floyd was involved in many other activities, including the ROTC. He also volunteered a lot of his time being a special assistant to me, the dean of students, and he assisted me in my duties as director of the TICEP program. I founded the program to give students a chance to give back to the community in the same manner that the school's founder, Booker T. Washington, helped organize the people in the community to support the school."

"There were twelve Black Belt counties that were under strict segregation laws in the state of Alabama, and these counties were among the poorest in the country. The program started out with a group of student - Floyd among them - who met on a Sunday afternoon in the gymnasium and discussed things everyone could do. The students agreed to participate in the program to make the counties a better place. The program started at five in the morning with exercises so that the students could participate before class. We started working with a variety of projects. In the beginning, there was not any funding, so we used my dean of student's budget to acquire some of the materials needed. The students - all volunteers - spent many hours getting out to the counties, even if they had to walk. Many students walked to tutor young people;, some helped repair home;, others gave lecture;, and the rest helped communities organize."

"The program started out with some 25 students, but during the early part of the summer, it increased to 300 students. By summer's end, they were up to 500. Students came back early to school to volunteer for the program, even though this meant leaving summer jobs and other responsibilities. The school was able to provide meals and free dorm rooms to such students during the summer. We applied for a grant from the Office of Economic Opportunity. Tuskegee Institute received the grant and the program grew to about 750 students. The grant allowed the program to pay the students a stipend and allowed them to work on getting transportation."

"The program became more sophisticated, offering formal programs of art, music, education, tutoring, health services, teacher training, community organization and

business development. This occurred in a span of three years. Floyd was involved at the beginning, when they were trying to get buses for the high-school students so that the college students could tutor them and pick them up to take them to various meeting places. Because of segregation, the bus companies would not rent to the school; therefore, we had to meet with the students and staff and collectively decided to go to Atlanta to the car-rental companies. The rental companies were national, so they could not discriminate the way the bus companies did. We ended up renting a fleet of cars from Avis, Hertz and National, and created a core of drivers and a transportation program. That's how we were able to move around. There was a director of transportation who was a student. The program eventually formed a series of student staff members that made sure the cars were maintained well and that the drivers followed all the rules—and this was before the days of seat belts."

"The students also helped organize an advisory committee in each of these counties. The committee worked with the TICEP tutors, who lived in homes in the communities, which allowed them to be a part of the community and contribute more than just tutoring. There were students from every walk of life and from various college majors. At that time, there was a major called Mechanical Industries, and there were students from that, as well."

"We were able to get Walter Ruther from United Auto Workers to donate two vehicles that were used as health wagons that the nursing and veterinarian students used to serve health needs. This activity became helpful health sessions that today are called health fairs. We also went into churches and communities to let them know the students were coming so that the people would come out for the health screenings. Once the screenings were finished, we would refer the patients to additional medical help at the John Andrews Hospital."

"The program also received food containers from donors. Floyd helped organize the trucks that took hot food out into the field to the students being tutored so that they could have meals. All of these efforts were led by students, and a number of the students became outstanding leaders. Floyd is one example; another is Patty Grave, who headed the Civilian Space Agency. Others include Judge Benton in Georgia and Roscoe Moore, who was an associate surgeon general for the United States. I gave a speech at St. Olaf College and, as a result of that, about 65 of the students from St.

Olaf came down and worked with the TICEP program. At this time, schools were still segregated, but students from St. Olaf and other colleges all across the U.S. came to help with the program. Floyd and I talked about our next move and began to work with John Brown, who was part of the program. We established another program that would take over once TICEP was finished. That program came into existence and stayed there as a community development program.

Floyd L. Griffin as scholar, ROTC Cadet Captain and Head Drum major.

WHO'S WHO IN AMERICAN COLLEGES AND UNIVERSITIES

Left to right-Front Row: Walter Bowers, Gwendolyn Patton, Willie Burnette. **Back Row:** Floyd Griffin, Roseda Marshall, Karen Gatewood, Earvin B. Aaron, Nettie Ball, Shirley Irick.

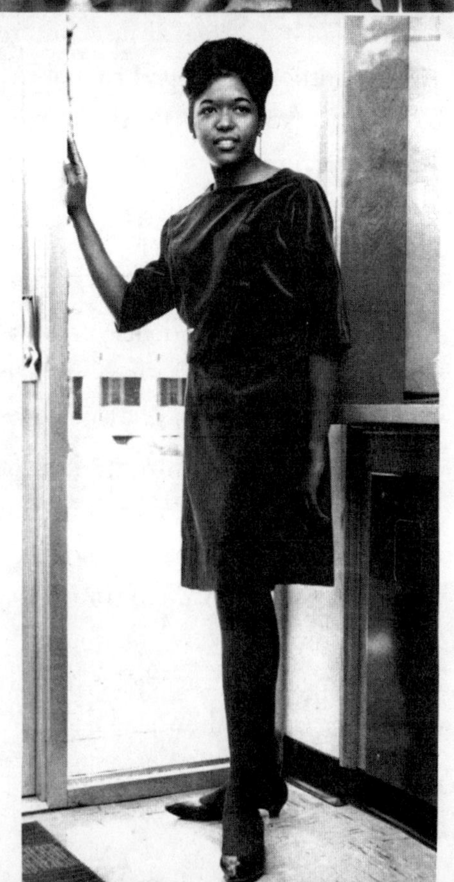

Nathalie Huffman
Tuskegee's Institute's Miss
United Methodist Congress.

STUDENT PROTESTS: A RISKY BUSINESS

One private concern I had was the impact that becoming involved in the student movement and possibly being arrested would have on my ability to join the military. However, my worry was in vain; I was never locked up, even though I participated in quite a few campaigns. I believed that injustice for any black person was an injustice against all blacks.

I recall one protest, in particular, in Montgomery at the State Capital, where the student contingent from Tuskegee, about two hundred strong, was surrounded and boxed in by local and state police who refused to allow us to leave our circle for hours on end. The police, some on horseback, most of them in riot gear, threatened to arrest anyone who broke away from group formation to use the restroom at Dexter Avenue Baptist Church or at the AME church down the street.

We had no other choice but to urinate outside where we stood. The authorities hoped to make things unbearable for us, and they tried to get from us as much information as they could about our identities and origin. If some of the protestors happened to be from Alabama, especially the Montgomery area, and their parents worked for the city or county or were business owners, the families became marked people and could expect a visit from the Jim Crow powers that be. Many of the students' parents were chastised by their employers, threatened with the loss of their jobs. Some had loans and mortgages called in by lien holders.

The unrest and confrontations persisted. Across the country, news accounts of police using dogs to attack protestors, and using blunt force against students and others, served up shameful televised scenes to a world audience. In some instances, the military was called out to quell the violence. Those were tumultuous times. I had not experienced a personal tragedy in the unrest—the death of someone I knew. But that changed on January 4, 1966.

Sammy Younge, one of my Tuskegee classmates, became the first student protestor to die in the Civil Rights Movement. I still remember vividly the January morning I learned the tragic news that Sammy had been killed. He lost his life for using a whites-only restroom at a gas station.

Sammy was an activist with SNCC, leading voter-registration campaigns with Stokely Carmichael, George and Wendy Paris, John Hewlett, John Jackson and others down in Lowndes County. His murder was a rude awakening for students at Tuskegee, and in response they marched on downtown Tuskegee in protest. Fired with indignation, the students registered to vote and joined the voter-registration drives in great numbers. We realized the need to identify candidates for public office who addressed the concerns of people of color, so later that year, young black activists helped to elect the first African American sheriff, Lucius Amerson, whose jurisdiction was Alabama's Macon County. I served Sheriff Amerson as a campaign worker in this history-making event. His victory was a symbol of the possibility of change in the South. But we received no victory in the courts for Sammy Younge. His murderer, a white man, was identified and brought to trial—and predictably acquitted in a Jim Crow courthouse. This act of injustice, and many others like it, galvanized the resolve of many, including me, to continue our goal of making the right to vote possible for the poor, rural residents of Macon, Lowndes and Dallas counties.

"Sammy's murder was a shocking experience," said Dr. Gwen Patton. "He was gunned down by a racist at a gas station for using the "whites only" restroom. He became the first college student killed in the Civil Rights Movement. His death brought us all to the reality that hateful and vicious acts were being committed against non-violent resistance without mercy. As you can imagine, parents were asking students to come home, to not be involved in marches any longer—you name it. Demonstrations took place in the city and around campus. There was a packed house at his funeral. People came out in the thousands. The leaders of all the black-liberation movements

attended his funeral. Nobody went to class for a couple of days. The Movement galvanized its strategies."

Patton continued. "As a result, Dr. P.B. Phillips started a program called the Tuskegee Institute Community Education Program, which was established to help the people in Alabama, especially in Macon and Lowndes Counties, to improve their educational level and quality of life from the standpoint of hygiene, eating habits, as well as tutorial programs. I was involved in the inception of the program, serving as the program coordinator. That led to a summer program where white students came down from the North, courageously came down, to spend a summer down there to work with SNCC, TICEP, the churches and others all over parts of Alabama. We had white and black kids driving around town registering voters. Their efforts and their presence infuriated the racist white folks. Our Northern white friends became open targets to brutality and death threats. This led to some relationships and marriages between blacks and whites. A couple of my friends ended up marrying white girls. That was just part of the Tuskegee experience."

"That was a time when you really could start seeing the possibilities of the country changing. You weren't totally sure but you could see some remnants of change. Our combined efforts gave the poor and oppressed people of the South some semblance of hope".

At that time, the city of Tuskegee had long experienced a divided black community. One segment was comprised of the privileged class, those well-educated elite who worked for the Institute and the well-paid administrators and doctors who worked for the Veterans Administration Hospital. Most lived in a beautiful and immaculate community in town and often did not socialize with poor blacks, who formed the other segment of the divided community. Sammy Younge belonged to one of the elite families. His father, a doctor, was head of the Department of Physical Medicine and Rehabilitation at the VA Hospital. His mother was the product of a well-to-do family from Charleston, South Carolina. Sammy was so fair-skinned he could pass for white. By the time I met him in college; he had attended Northern boarding schools and spoke like a Northerner. During that time, it was customary for black privileged families to send their children to private, integrated schools in the North. Some of these parents were teachers in segregated Southern schools that grossly lacked sufficient funds, supplies and facilities, and they did not want their children to suffer such disparities. However, these privileged-class parents reconnected their children with the black community by enrolling them in a black college, most often a parent's alma mater. In Sammy's case, it was a given that he would follow in the footsteps of his father—at least, in one respect—by attending Tuskegee. At Tuskegee, he was a mechanical and industrial arts major.

Those who knew Sammy were not surprised by the act of rebellion that led to his death. Throughout his life, Sammy had boldly defied authority. His parents discouraged him from socializing with children of working-class parents, but Sammy befriended many of the children from the poor black part of town. They became his playmates when he returned home after having been expelled from the boarding school to which his family had sent him. In addition to defying his family's rules of acceptable behavior for the elite, Sammy openly challenged his professors at Tuskegee and questioned the rules of the college. He went to Montgomery, well-dressed and well-spoken, to act as a patron of unassuming white merchants who did not know he was black—a dangerous thing to do, given the times and circumstances, but that was Sammy's way of mocking the rules of Jim Crow.

After Sammy's death, all roads seemed to lead to Tuskegee, as civil-rights leaders, activists, members of the press, and grieving students attended his memorial service. The Tuskegee senior class dedicated the 1966 yearbook to Sammy's memory. His death was a grim reminder to us of the viciousness of our detractors. Suddenly, we had joined the ranks of other Southern cities that had become scenes of murder in the struggle.

A Garden in Which to Grow

Tuskegee Institute was the perfect setting for me to grow personally and professionally. In addition to coursework, students were encouraged, and often required, to participate in activities that broadened our cultural understanding of the world. Like most young college students, I balked when I learned I had to go to chapel during freshman and sophomore years. But to my surprise, chapel featured some of the greatest leaders of our time—people like CORE's James Farmer, the NAACP's Medgar Evers, Dr. Martin Luther King, Jr., and Malcolm X. We had another auditorium program called Vespers, a Sunday evening event of arts and entertainment that included performances from opera and ballet companies, and lecturers of note. My alma mater offered these and other quality-of-life experiences that I wish I had valued then as much as I do now.

The extracurricular activities at Tuskegee contributed to a well-rounded experience. I became a dedicated participant in its ROTC program, one of the most respected in the country. I played the clarinet and later became the head drum major for the college band, which performed during sellout crowds at Tuskegee football games. At that time, the Tuskegee Tigers held the record for having the most winning seasons of any HBCU. Our track team, of which I was a member, was legendary also.

A major factor in the students' growth at Tuskegee was the encouragement we received from distinguished professors. I was particularly impressed by a history professor, a white gentleman named Dr. Stallings. He was a brilliant man who often taught without using any class notes. Instead, he eloquently lectured from memory for almost an hour. He recognized each of his students, recalling us by name wherever we were, and would hold us accountable for being diligent in our academic pursuits. His gift of recall and dedication had a tremendous impact on me. I sought his advice when trying to select the subjects I needed in order to be successful in and out of the classroom. I also used to go back to campus and talk to him about topics unrelated to class. He always welcomed the intrusion and often challenged me to try and consider an argument from the opposing perspective.

However, the best thing I took away from Tuskegee was Nathalie Elaine Huffman, the woman who would become my wife. Nathalie was a reserved, focused young beauty from Birmingham, Alabama, who caught my attention immediately. She impressed me so much that it wasn't long before I felt I could not live without her. We were students together, worked in the movement together, risked our lives in protests together, graduated, and married. Forty-two years, two sons, six grand-children, fourteen moves and a military career later, my feelings for her are still the same: I can't live without her.

Reflections from Nathalie

Floyd and I met during the second semester of my junior year at Tuskegee Institute—it was "institute" at that time; it was not yet called "university." And actually, I had a choice between two colleges. One was Talladega, and the other was Tuskegee. Tuskegee's scholarship was a little more than Talladega's, and that's how I ended up choosing the school. Had I not done so, maybe Floyd and I would not have met. So maybe there was some great plan at work for both of our lives.

Tuskegee Institute was located in one of the poorest counties in Alabama. Despite its general location Tuskegee has always had an excellent academic reputation and I was very excited about becoming a student there. There was not much of a downtown area of Tuskegee. Downtown Tuskegee had few shops, and the black students were advised not to go there. The college was basically an oasis in a big barren country area. Students looked forward to receiving care packages from home.

Tuskegee students, I am proud to say, were very much involved in the Civil Rights Movement. We marched, we protested, but most of all, we reached out to people in surrounding communities who were in need. We tutored students, repaired homes, collected books to be distributed to under privileged families and did whatever we could to make their lives better. I'm not too sure that we were all that aware of the dangers that were involved. We had a belief... a desire... we took a stand... and we acted.

I am originally from Birmingham, so I remember riding on the segregated buses which had signs that read whites only, on this side, and colored section, on the other. White people during this time could take any seat they wanted to on the bus, even if it was on the black side. Another significant thing that happened in Birmingham was the bombing at the Sixteenth Street Baptist Church that occurred in 1963, where the four little girls died. Although I was away at school at the time, this tragedy set the stage for the Movement all over the world. The Sixteenth Street Baptist Church bombing; the use of fire hoses and police dogs on demonstrators; those were tragedies that shined a light worldwide on so much that had been kept in the dark.

I can remember my parents' determination to exercise their right to vote in Birmingham. They were not college graduates; they had elementary school educations, but they still had to memorize and interpret parts of the Constitution and pay a poll tax in order to be allowed to vote. I remember asking myself, "Why is it that blacks are not good enough? Why does everything have to be different for us?" In other words, Why the double standard? But they never missed the opportunity to vote in every election. Having the privilege to vote meant so much to them.

My father, Gaston Huffman, worked for L&N, better known as the Louisville and Nashville Railroad. It operated freight and passenger services in the southeast United States. The company was located in Birmingham. He worked there for 35 years before he retired. He was an oiler for about 20 years. When the trains would come into the yard, he would crawl underneath the boxcars to oil the wheels on the cars, which was a very dangerous job. Daddy was later promoted to a journeyman, and with this new position he would repair the train cars. My mother was a beautician, and she had her own shop called Mikki's Beauty Shop, located in our home. Her name is Charlotte Gratton, but her nickname is Mikki. She retired after being in business 30 years.

SLATER'S FUNERAL HOME: A FAMILY AFFAIR

Slater's Funeral Home was established in 1911 and was one of the few undertaking businesses in our region of the state. When I was growing up, Slater's was the only predominantly black funeral home in our locale. This remained so until the mid-1950s. The establishment was owned by the Slater family until my parents and Professor Joseph Graham, the high-school principal, acquired the business in 1966. By then, the 55-year-old institution had lost the glory of its early years, since there were no local surviving Slater relatives to maintain its legacy. When Professor Graham died in 1969, my parents became the sole owners of the historic business, and they worked ardently to restore its luster. They moved Slater's from its original location, three or four doors down the street on the same block, to its current location at 244 N. Wayne Street. They revitalized the operation, bringing it back to a high level of service and quality.

The late Mrs. Marie Williams, office manager of Slater's, was an important dedicated fixture in the business who became a great friend of our family. Mr. Samuel Thomas worked with the newly acquired business as a part-time funeral director. He also helped us tremendously during the transition period, as we became familiar with operating the business. Over the years, there have been others who have worked at Slater's and been much a part of its growth and history. They include Leslie Wilcher, office manager; Marilyn Gordon, assistant office manager; and Mamie Worthen, Donald Pinkston, Robert Mallory, Henry Simmons, Bennie Evans, Harry Zachary, James Jones, Joseph Foreman, Bobby Knox, James Brown, Henry Allen, Henry Willis, Marshall Boyer, James Kay, Tommy Knox, Willetta Stanley, Johnny Pinkston, Michael Pinkston, Laura and James Young, Terry Sheppard, Johnny Cook and Diaz Steele.

Today, Slater's is the second oldest funeral home in Milledgeville and is a partner to area churches and the community at large. Slater's is part of an illustrious African American history, having served the community continually for 98 years. In 2011, we will celebrate its centennial. Institutions such as Slater's, because they are record keepers of historical family events, are important resources in the community. They are also one of the few remaining independent major businesses that still exist in the black community. This is one key reason I felt proud to be a member of the staff of Slater's Funeral Home when Nathalie and I retired from our military journey and returned home.

Slater's Funeral Home, Inc.

"A Tradition

Mrs. Ruth Evans Griffin, Chairman of the Board
Floyd L. Griffin JR, President * Funeral Director* Embalmer
Mrs. Delbra Griffin Waller, First Vice-President * Secretary* Treasurer* Funeral Director* Insurance Agent
Toney Griffin, 2nd Vice-President* Assist Secretary & Treasurer

Chapter 4

Uncle Sam, But No Uncle Tom
Military Years and College Assignments

1967 – Commissioned as a 2nd Lieutenant in the US Army, I was assigned to the Engineer Officer's Basic Course at Ft. Belvoir, VA. While waiting for my paperwork to be processed I worked as a Chief Estimator and Planner for Atkinson Brothers Construction Company in Atlanta, GA. Nathalie and I were newly married. She worked as a professor's assistant at Tuskegee as we started our life together. Brian, our first son was born in Birmingham.

Following a three month training program at Ft. Belvoir, I was assigned to the 339th Engineering Battalion at Ft. Lewis, Washington. Nathalie and I packed up our belongings and traveled across the country to the Pacific Rim-Puget Sound area, a 2,500 mile trip. Ft. Lewis has one of the largest and most modern military reservations in the United States. We lived in an apartment off post that was first rate. We were extremely happy to know we could receive first-rate medical care through Madigan Army Medical Center because Eric, our second son, was on the way.

When Dr. Martin Luther King, Jr., was murdered on April 4, 1968, I was stationed at Fort Lewis, Tacoma, Washington. My unit was on alert due to the rioting that occurred in some one hundred cities around the country. Many of my fellow officers were hoping that our unit would not have to go out to control the unrest. Though we had an obligation to the military, the black officers and soldiers were conflicted, for we understood the frustration of those rioters—we, too, were angry about the violent death of a man who represented nonviolence, inclusion and peace.

Ft. Lewis was my first assignment as a newly commissioned officer, and I remained there for a year. Admittedly, I had mixed emotions when I went in, for I wasn't sure if I wanted a career in the Army. I was married and had a young son so I questioned any decision that would affect my family, including the military. At that time, during the late sixties, the future seemed promising for blacks in the military. The Army, wanting to demonstrate how colorblind and inclusive it could be, began to go out of its way to create opportunities for black officers and soldiers. Therefore, my options as a new officer were quite expansive.

My platoon was involved in building a training site for soldiers assigned to Vietnam. Fort Lewis was also the ROTC training center for the Advanced Basic Camp. I became part of the teaching staff at the ROTC Advanced Basic Camp. This was a period when the Army aggressively demonstrated the desire to be more diverse. It seemed that whatever your interest, the Army was willing to give qualified candidates the opportunity. A flight school opportunity became available and I applied, passed the battery of tests and was chosen to enter flight school at Army Primary Helicopter School, Ft. Wolters, Texas. I was the only Black officer in my section of 25 students. We learned to fly the TH-55, the OH-23 and the OH-13 during the twenty week training camp. I graduated in the top 10% of the class. The second phase of helicopter training was conducted at the US Army Aviation Center, Ft. Rucker, Alabama. That was welcome news because we would be close to our family. Everyone was excited to see the new baby.

Reflections from Nathalie

Floyd and I were married on June 15, 1966, in Columbus, Georgia. I graduated in August of that year with a degree in Biology and worked for a year on campus in the School of Veterinary Medicine. Floyd graduated the following year and our first son, Brian, was born shortly before Floyd went on active duty in the military.

I did not hold many full-time jobs because we moved so often early in his career. I have often said if I had known I was going to marry someone who wanted a life in the military, I probably would have become a nurse or a teacher because it was easier to get jobs in those fields. By the time he retired, we had moved fourteen times in 23 years. I don't regret any of it because I would not have seen so many different places and had so many rewarding experiences, were it not for my life with Floyd.

His first active duty assignment was at Fort Lewis in the state of Washington. I'll never forget, my parents said we looked like the Beverly Hillbillies when we left on that trip because we had everything we owned packed in or on that car. We had a luggage carrier that was attached to the roof of the car. It was cram packed and the baby's crib was attached to that. It took us seven days to drive from Alabama to the state of Washington. Our second son, Eric, was born in Tacoma, Washington during that assignment.

From Washington, we went to Mineral Wells, Texas for four-and-a half months, then we spent another five months in Fort Rucker, Alabama so that Floyd could complete his flight school training. Following flight school, he was sent to Alexandria, Virginia, which was the first of three assignments he had in the Washington, D.C. area. For most of his military career, Floyd was the first black officer to serve, or the only black officer serving his unit which meant that I was the first or only black officer's wife.

I would attend luncheons, coffees and other officer's wives' activities. But I also became a very active volunteer in whichever community we were living in at the time. I was always involved with our children's schools and our local churches. In addition, over the years I have volunteered with the Red Cross, the Knight Foundation, Morgan County, GA Cultural Center, Convention & Visitors Bureau, Grassroots Art Program and Adult Education programs. Those experiences made me aware of other cultures and enriched my life and hopefully those of others.

I think the most rewarding assignment for me was when Floyd was stationed at Fort Stewart, Georgia and commanded a battalion. As a commander's wife, I had the opportunity to be involved with the wives of junior officers, non-commissioned officers, and enlisted men. The battalion chaplain and I set up various programs, activities and counseling to assist families in times of deployment. We wanted to be sure that families were well cared for so that soldiers could perform their jobs without distractions.

At Ft. Rucker I learned to fly larger helicopters like the Huey, used in combat, rescue and general transport of troops and supplies. After five months of intense training I earned my wings. My first assignment as a pilot was at Davidson Army Airfield, Ft Belvoir, VA. My job was to transport high ranking officers, dignitaries and government officials around the Washington, DC area. One of my most memorable passengers was General William C. Westmoreland, Army Chief of Staff. During this six month assignment I also commanded a Engineer training company at Ft. Belvoir, the Engineer School. In preparation for new duties in Vietnam, I went back to Ft. Rucker and attended the Instructor Pilot's Training Program, becoming a certified instructor pilot; able to fly, test a pilot's proficiency on certain aircraft, and teach at the flight school.

It was the first time I had ever been outside the United States for a long period of time. Serving in Vietnam was hard, a radically different experience. The first thing I noticed was the odor, some of which came from burning human waste. There was the problem of getting adjusted to a daily routine of working very long hours, seven days a week, for an entire year. I was assigned to the 227th Assault Helicopter Battalion as a Battalion Intelligence Officer (S-2). I also served as an instructor pilot. I evaluated all helicopter pilots to test their efficiency in operating combat and transport helicopters. I led and flew on several combat missions.

The Vietnam War was a guerilla operation, not a conventional war like World War I or II. This meant that action could occur any time, anywhere. The other helicopter pilots and I were not exempt from danger; we flew to different operations areas with the understanding that we could be fired upon at any moment. But the experience wasn't all bad—we ate well most of the time.

My other responsibility was that of Commander of the 93rd Construction Engineering Company. I was A Company Commander. My responsibility was to manage the inventory of all major equipment coming in country. My company constructed roads and managed the sand and cement processing plant that created sand cement to stabilize landing strips and roads. We also placed miles and miles of asphalt.

We occasionally enjoyed entertainment that included a visit from the entertainers. I met the then-reigning Miss Black America. I was chosen to fly her around the sector that we were operating. I was thrilled to learn that she was from Birmingham, Alabama, my wife's hometown. I asked her to contact my family when she returned to Alabama, and she did just that. Imagine my surprise when I returned to the states and ran into her in downtown Birmingham. It's amazing how small the world is.

I don't often talk about the time I spent in Vietnam, because it wasn't the best time of my life. I had some good friends who lost their lives there. Others returned, physically and mentally wounded. But one thing I've learned is that you should never allow the past to adversely control your present and negatively impact your future. So even though I lived through the nightmare of Vietnam, I still have appreciation and gratitude for having had the opportunity to work with good people who gave much—and in some cases, the ultimate sacrifice—to their country. I'm grateful for that. Furthermore, my service in Vietnam helped me to take advantage of professional opportunities. The war was an asset on my resume, lending credibility to my pursuits as the military noted favorably my service. Therefore, as bitter as it was, my Vietnam tour factored greatly in helping me to accomplish what I did in my twenty-three years in the Army.

Following my tour of duty in Vietnam I was assigned to US Army, J. F. K. Center for Military Assistance, Ft Bragg, NC, as Operations Staff Officer from 1971–1972. Assignments where I could have my family with me helped provide a true quality of life existence. I worked closely with the Interested Officers Association, and became its president. It was a community focused leadership group that promoted good will and professional development for its officers. We brought in heavyweight champion Joe Frazier to one of our special programs. It was a highly publicized event.

In 1973 I entered the Engineer Officers' Advance Course at Ft. Belvoir, VA, a 9 month course. I also pursued a Master's degree in contract procurement management at Florida Institute of Technology in Melbourne, FL in 1974.

My next assignment was as ROTC Officer at two North Carolina Universities, Wake Forest and Winston Salem State University, to share the benefits of ROTC and gain more participation. Army ROTC is one of the best leadership courses in the country and should be a part of all college curriculum. I am a living example of how learning to become a leader will make your college experience even richer-and prepare you for the future. These are the results I sought. It was an interesting challenge. At Winston-Salem State I represented a major gateway to a solution to the financial burdens facing many Black college students. I immediately talked to the coaches of the football and basketball teams because they had firsthand knowledge of players who were slipping academically and some whose athletic scholarships were in jeopardy. They were most gracious and impressed with my accomplishments as an officer, a war hero and a leader.

I was the first African American assigned to the military-science department at Wake Forest University in Winston-Salem, North Carolina. I started an ROTC program at Winston-Salem State University (WSSU) and coached on two undefeated football teams there. It was the best four years of my entire military career.

When I arrived, Wake Forest already had an ROTC program in place, and the Winston-Salem program was in its infancy. I was chosen to work at both—at Wake Forest, a predominantly white college with a Baptist influence, and Winston-Salem, a predominantly black state university. I also started an ROTC program at a private institution, Highpoint College in Highpoint, North Carolina. The Army agreed to support WSSU's effort to develop an ROTC presence on its campus, but not as a separate program, which can be costly to set up. Instead, WSSU's ROTC became an expansion program of Wake Forest University.

It took serious creative recruiting to stimulate student interest in ROTC at Wake Forest and Winston-Salem. One of the tools we used was the offer of full scholarships. My willingness to volunteer to coach the offensive backfield of the football team of Winston–Salem State University helped me in building the ROTC, because many of the recruits came from the athletic program. Some of those young men went into the advanced ROTC program, received their commissions, and did well in the military. More than a few consider me a mentor, and they call and talk to me about what they're doing today. Some have retired but still call to ask if they can use my name to get a post-military job. I am very proud of that.

I almost made Winston-Salem my permanent home because my sons had gotten involved in the community and my wife enjoyed the area. When we lived there, it was a quaint, small, intimate city with many wonderful people who have become lifelong friends.

"We've known the Griffins for 35 years, a professional relationship that grew to a great friendship as we consider them family as well as friends," says retired Lt. Colonel William Mezyck. Mrs. Mezyck adds, "Floyd has been like an older brother to my older children and like a father to my younger children. He and Nathalie's friendship certainly has added quality to our life. We were stationed in Europe together and raised each other's children in a wholesome, loving atmosphere. William, in recalling their days together, says, "Floyd has always been a leader and a mentor to the younger

generation. We've maintained the closest relationship that I had with anyone in the Army. He is an individual of excellent character who handles matters professionally at all times. I was a little disappointed when he decided not to pursue the position that would place him on track to become General because I knew that had he remained, he would surely have achieved that goal too. He's just that kind of guy.

Coaching Legends

There was a coach at Wake Forest University whom I came to know very well. After my first semester at the school, this coach left Wake Forest to lead the program at Winston-Salem State University. I offered my services and he asked me to become part of his coaching staff. Yes, I had played running back when I was in high school, but I didn't know anything about coaching when he offered me the job. But his faith in me, and his ability to discern the merits of an individual, is part of the reason why Coach Bill Hayes became a great friend.

To chronicle the thirty-nine-year athletics career of Bill Hayes would take volumes. Currently, he is director of athletics at Florida A&M University. Before that, he made a name for himself as director of athletics at North Carolina Central University (NCCU), a school from which he graduated in 1965. Hayes spent a total of twenty-seven years as head football coach of two of NCCU's biggest rivals, Winston-Salem State University and North Carolina A&T. He became a pioneer in the desegregation of the Atlantic Coast Conference's coaching ranks when Wake Forest University hired him as an offensive-line coach in 1973. He also had eight successful years as a high-school coach in football, basketball and track, his teams winning state championships. In his position at NCCU, Hayes used his experience in public relations and fundraising to make improvements to the athletic department. His 195-102-2 record as a college coach suggests that his techniques for motivating people are successful and will work to his advantage in his newest assignment at Florida A&M.

"When I met Floyd—at that time he was Captain Griffin, and all of the players called him "Cap"—he wanted to build the best ROTC program in the Carolinas, and knowing Floyd, he probably wanted to build the best program in the nation," said Hayes. "He was smart enough to realize that we had the best candidates for military service right on our football team because they were bigger, stronger, faster and smarter than any of the other kids around... and he felt that with his help, we had the ability to put all four of those qualities together. And so Floyd came to me and asked me to let him help me coach. At first I thought he was kidding, but soon I discovered that he was dead serious. Having no prior college coaching experience, I trained Floyd session by session, day by day. We stayed one day ahead of our practice schedule at first, getting him ready to do his job as a coach."

"Floyd did an unbelievable job in training our running backs. He had a real gift. His military service and military-leadership training made him a natural coach. The first thing he thought we had to have was good solid discipline and attention to detail, a quality he was very good at. He started with the simplicity of a stance, and how to properly take a hand-off, and we did it fundamentally, day-by-day. At each practice there were two things we were going to try to accomplish that day. We went from two things the first day, to four things the second day, and eight things the third day, and then we repeated those. In just a short while, he was teaching eight things a day and a solid routine."

"After a short amount of time, Floyd had trained himself, along with my help, to be a real good coach. Our players really responded to him and he was worth his

weight in gold in teaching leadership and discipline. He taught a lot of positive things when it came to making a guy a better football player and a better person. I think he had two or three or four of his running backs who went on to play in the NFL, and they still love him today. So, the guy was not only a good leader and builder of men, he was a real good coach and one of the best friends I have ever had in my life. And that relationship goes on to this day. His learning curve was extremely fast. In fact, after we made it through that first year—I think we might have been 11and 0—Floyd came to me asking if I would let him run the offense the next year. So, if you can believe that someone would learn that fast and be that confident in himself, and be that bold and brash, then that was Floyd Griffin."

"I wouldn't want to leave out that, as a result of Floyd's involvement with our football team and coaching our running backs, players from all of our positions started gravitating towards Floyd. The numbers in the ROTC kept growing. When we started, we probably had one or two kids in the ROTC. I imagine by the time he had been there two years, three-fourths of the team was in the ROTC. Also, something happened during the summer months that we did not expect; we got better as a team because Floyd kept our players in condition. He trained with them and took them to Fort Bragg to participate in the military competitions. I would go down with him sometimes to the competitions because all of my players were going. And we won all of those events down at Bragg with flying colors, which made us the number-one ROTC program that participated, and probably made us the best ROTC program in the country."

"Winston-Salem State athletics gained a lot from having Floyd Griffin around. Our student athletes learned important qualities of manhood under his direction, thanks to his leadership qualities, his desire, and his character. As a result, our ROTC ended up growing. And a result of all of that: a lot of those players went on to play professional ball and became leaders and career military guys. Some generals even came out of that crowd. Floyd Griffin left his mark on that program, setting a standard for years to come."

Coach Gaines with All American Earl "the Pearl" Monroe who went on to become an NBA legend. players.

CLARENCE "BIG HOUSE" GAINES

Clarence E. "Big House" Gaines, Sr. was born in Paducah, Kentucky. He attended the public schools of Paducah and graduated in 1941, as class salutatorian, from Paducah's Lincoln High School. He excelled academically, played basketball, and was an All State football player. While at Morgan State Gaines received recognition as an All-American football player and participated on the basketball and track teams. Gaines graduated from Morgan State in 1945 with a B.S. degree in Chemistry intent on furthering his education and attending dental school.

During Coach Gaines[1] 47-year tenure as coach and athletic director at Winston-Salem State University he coached former WSSU and professional basketball greats Cleo Hill (first African American from an historically Black college and university to be drafted #1 by the National Basketball Association -- St. Louis Hawks, 1961) and Earl "The Pearl" Monroe (pictured above), Naismith Basketball Hall of Fame inductee and all star performer) of the National Basketball Association's New York Knicks.

Upon his retirement as basketball coach at Winston-Salem State University in 1993, Gaines had amassed a win/loss record of 828-446, making him the most winning active basketball coach in NCAA history, and the second most winning collegiate basketball coach behind the University of Kentucky's late Adolph Rupp. However, following University of North Carolina basketball coach Dean Smith's 877th career win in March 1997, coach Gaines became the third most winning basketball coach in NCAA history behind only Adolph Rupp (2nd), and Dean Smith (1st).

Coach Gaines imparting wisdom to friendship to his players.

Me and "Big House"

The people I have come across throughout my life have shaped my destiny in many ways. There is an old saying that *"people come into our lives for a reason, a season or a lifetime."*

When I first came to Winston Salem State University as the ROTC instructor, one of the first people that I was introduced to was Clarence "Big House" Gaines. From that time until the time that I left Winston-Salem for my next assignment, I felt very blessed that I could call him my friend knowing that I could look to him for advice about anything. Looking back, I am glad that he came into my life. He influenced my thoughts and actions then and still I think of him fondly.

I think he was just as happy to share our relationship. He often expressed to me how good it was to have a military figure; a black officer, who definitely served as a very positive role model for his basketball players, as well as other students on campus. It was clear that the influence I had on students went a long way in the development of the students' understanding of "leadership". As I traveled over the campus, I befriended many students, not just my ROTC students. They looked up to me and often would seek my advice and let me know of their own accomplishments, knowing that I would have a word of encouragement for them. I had the opportunity to speak to many student groups during several university programs. A theme that I often preached was one that I have carried with me throughout my life; and that is the theme of "being a winner." Friends could always expect me to share with them my trademark, "Winners make it happen."

Big House's friendship was very important to me, and I soon came to realize also how important I was to him. Big House often invited me to travel with him when he went on trips to recruit basketball talent to WSSU. I know that he wanted his players to be outstanding in every way, and my status as a black officer went a long way to instill

Big House's values into his players. It went without saying that he expected excellence from all of his players; not only on the court, but in all that they did. As a result, his players were on their best behavior on campus as well as on the court.

I often helped him out by mentoring some of his players. We both expected excellence, and I think that is what led to our mutual respect for one another and what we wanted to instill in our students....my ROTC students as well as his players.

I felt honored when he thought enough of me to include my wife and I as guests at his daughter's wedding. It was a very exclusive and lavish affair. We had developed a relationship that I would cherish for many years. His death was a great loss for all the many players he influenced, the friends he made, and the contribution to manhood he represented.

It was a very sad occasion for me when I returned to Winston-Salem for his funeral in 2005. Hearing of his death caused me to stop and think of the legacy that he had left with all who knew him, and that I had been blessed to share a friendship with this great man. His death was a blow to all who knew him; knowing what he had been to me, it went without saying that I would make arrangements to travel back for the final rites. As I sat and observed the crowd of mourners who attended the funeral, it was a definite indication of how many lives he had touched. Players he had influenced throughout the years were in attendance, including the most famous of his players, Earl "the Pearl" Monroe. The mayor of the city and many other dignitaries whose lives had been touched by this great man were also present; I felt just as important as any of them, because that is how he made everyone feel.

Reflections from my Student Athletes

Robert Weeks:

(Robert Weeks is today a Lieutenant Colonel U. S. Army (retired)

"When I first met Floyd Griffin in 1976, he was a captain in the U.S. Army serving at Wake Forest University as an assistant professor of military science, and I was a junior enrolled at Winston-Salem State University. We referred to him as "Cap." I first became acquainted with Cap when he asked Coach Bill Hayes if he could assist with coaching. Hayes was the head football coach at WSSU and was in his first year."

"Coach Hayes shared with me the story of how the conversation went between him and Cap. When Cap asked Coach Hayes whether he could become an assistant coach, Hayes asked him where he played college football and Cap responded that he did not play college football. Hayes asked him where he played high-school football and Cap responded that he played high-school football in his hometown of Milledgeville. Hayes then responded, "You want to help me coach at a Division II school and you haven't coached or played college football?" Cap explained to Bill Hayes that what he could offer is leadership, experience in how to conduct physical conditioning, and his ability to learn new ideas and concepts quickly. Hayes decided to take a chance with Cap; after all, he really didn't have anything to lose. Cap began his coaching career as coach of the running backs. Every day, Coach Hayes would teach him one technique until Cap had learned everything he needed to coach the running backs. Cap began to learn new things on his own as well."

"Shortly after starting his coaching duties, Cap began to recruit some of the football players into the Army ROTC program at Wake Forest (which we later found out was Cap's ulterior motive). I and some of my teammates decided to check out the ROTC program. At that time, cadets were paid a $100 monthly stipend for signing a contract to accept a commission as a second lieutenant upon graduation, and I needed the money. But it was Cap's persuasive attitude that made me sign up. I was majoring in health and physical education, and at the beginning of my junior year of college had realized that I had chosen an academic major that I really did not want to pursue as a career. Joining ROTC would give me another career choice, and

if I didn't like it, I could simply terminate my contract as soon as I served my initial obligation of four years."

"Once I decided to join ROTC, I had one problem to overcome: I did not have the prerequisites to enter the senior ROTC course. To be eligible, I had to have completed one of the following: 1) 2 years of high-school ROTC; 2) at least 2 years of ROTC my freshman and sophomore years in college (basic course); 3) basic training on active duty; 4) service on active duty; 5) an assignment to a National Guard or Reserve unit; or 6) the ROTC Basic Course at Fort Knox, Kentucky, between my sophomore and junior years of college."

"Cap figured out a way to get the prerequisite waived. That required me to meet with the professor of military science, or the PMS, at Wake Forest and convince him that I had the potential to serve as a second lieutenant in the U.S. Army. To say the least, I was a nervous wreck going in before a lieutenant colonel. I remember Cap preparing me prior to going in to see the PMS, which eased my nerves and made it much easier to present the argument about why I should be enrolled in the senior ROTC program in one of the most prestigious programs in the country. I was amazed to find that the PMS was willing to waive all prerequisites. I believe it had much more to do with Cap's credibility and professionalism than with me convincing the PMS. In return, I had to pledge that I would give a 100 percent commitment in making up what I had missed by not having one of the prerequisites."

"At the end of my junior year, I had successfully completed the ROTC Advanced Camp at Fort Bragg with a very good rating. I was promoted to cadet lieutenant colonel my senior year, the highest rank at WSSU, and I graduated as a Distinguished Military Graduate (DMG). I could not have achieved all of these accomplishments without the assistance and mentoring of Captain Griffin. Cap had a way of motivating everyone that was under his control. He would not accept a mediocre performance if he knew you were not giving your all. He inspired me to at least look at active military service, largely because of the way he carried himself. He was a positive role model for me and others to emulate. Prior to graduating in 1978, I asked for active military service. Because I was a DMG, I could have asked for Reserve duty and probably would have gotten it. But I wanted to follow in Cap's footsteps."

"After being commissioned, I decided that I would evaluate the first four years of service before deciding whether to make the Army a career. Once I got on active duty, I felt as though I was prepared to meet the rigorous demands of serving on active duty. Cap had challenged us while in ROTC and gave us the skills we needed to be successful. He also gave me personal values, such as pride in my work, being prepared mentally as well as physically, having confidence in my abilities, and learning how to develop short-term, mid-term and long-term goals for myself."

"After I began my career, I crossed paths with Cap several times, and he has remained a mentor and friend. I know that Cap made a positive impact on who I am today. I owe a great deal of my professional development and success to Cap. I still use the skills he taught me when I develop my subordinates. During my military career, I served on two college campuses, teaching senior ROTC. I patterned my leadership style from what I learned from Cap. I also applied his technique of recruiting ROTC cadets from the sporting teams by volunteering to coach various teams on campus. As a result, I was successful in meeting my recruiting mission and retaining quality athletes who had the same qualities the U.S. Army was looking for in its leaders."

"Cap taught me that even if you don't have the skills to complete a task, [you should] maintain a positive attitude and develop a plan. He walked onto a Division II football team with absolutely no experience, and coached one of the best running backs in NFL history, Timmy Newsome, who played nine seasons with the world-champion Dallas Cowboys. Cap coached other running backs that played semi-professional football, became high-school principals, and are successful in other careers. I attained the rank of lieutenant colonel and several others attained the same rank, or higher. If I had to sum up Cap's legacy, I would say he is a small man in stature who made a huge impact on the lives of the many he developed."

Mooresville, North Carolina, school-system administrator Randy Bolton remembers Griffin vividly and with fondness.

"Cap coached me as a running back at Winston-Salem State University from 1976 to 1979. I was a young man and I observed how dedicated and organized he was—always on time. We [the players] worked hard and sometimes we would complain about how hard it was. He would quickly remind us of who we were. He

Newsome says that he was always amazed by Griffin's coaching skills.

showed us how to persevere, how to get over the issues and keep going, keep striving."

Randy is quick to credit Floyd Griffin with the traits that have helped him succeed.

"His organizational skills helped me throughout college. I took the dedication and strategies he showed us to my own career. He taught me that I could do anything. I went on to get a master's degree and then my doctorate. Many times, I wanted to give up, but I remembered how he pushed us to persevere. He'll never realize the impact he had on my life."

FORMER DALLAS COWBOY RUNNING BACK TIMMY NEWSOME REMEMBERS GRIFFIN WITH APPRECIATION.

"Cap taught me to think positive in the face of adversity. He gave me the necessary impetus to endure and move forward, even when things didn't seem as rosy as they appeared."

"He never played college football. I thought it was remarkable that he could understand and teach the game so well. He consistently created outstanding players out of individuals with various backgrounds, transforming us into men in a very short time. In fact, because of his military leadership, quite a few of the guys I knew off the field now have successful military careers."

MILITARY COLLEGES

After completing ROTC at Wake Forest and Winston Salem Universities, I attended the **United States Army Command & General Staff College**. This is a prestigious institution available to accomplished officers on the road to consideration as full Colonels and Generals. The college educates and trains intermediate level Army Officers, International Officers, and Interagency leaders for preparation in a full spectrum of Army, joint, interagency, and multinational operations. My first assignment at Army Command & General Staff was to the 18th Engineer Brigade in West Germany as Brigade Logistics Staff Officer S4. In this position, my duties included advising and assisting the Commander in planning and executing everything involved with the logistical, or supply, issues of the brigade. A tremendous responsibility, I dove in and gave it all I had. Distribution and budget were a large part of the assignment and I successfully managed a $6 million logistics budget. I also became actively involved with our unit's flag football team, the German/American Volksfests. Lieutenant Colonel Gene C. Rizer, Deputy Commander, had these remarks to make: *"Major Griffin was responsible for publishing a new Brigade Logistics Standard Operations Procedure (SOP) that serves as the single source document for the operation of the entire brigade logistics program. He developed and published specific procedures for the control of the logistics budget which has improved the accountability of logistics funds."*

My next assignment in Germany was to the 79th Engineer Battalion as Battalion Executive Officer (2nd in command of the battalion). Here, I also carried out a number of duties including, but not limited to, directing, supervising, and coordinating all actions of the battalion staff, insuring that the Commander's directives were carried out completely and thoroughly. I also served as the Logistics Readiness Officer, the Fund Certifying Officer (managing a budget of over $2.4 million) and as the Deputy Installation Coordinator of Gerszewski Barracks, a 2,220-man installation. When necessary, I served in the Commander's position during any absences.

My last assignment in Germany before returning to the states was as Director of Engineering and Housing (DEH) of the Military Community at Karlsrube (Germany). As the first African American to hold this position, I managed 9 million square feet of property that encompassed 13,500 total personnel, including 456 civilian and military staff. I managed a budget of over $35 million and served in the additional capacities of Fire Marshal, Master Planner, Stationing Officer, Environmental/Energy Conservation Officer, and Community Remote Site Coordinator. While serving as DEH on this assignment, I was promoted to Lieutenant Colonel by Colonel Charles Williams.

We had traveled to Germany in the anticipation of my serving for 3 years, but we ended up staying an extra year for professional purposes. My children thoroughly enjoyed the stay, having had the opportunity to travel throughout Europe. One of my most memorable events during our time there was my 40th birthday. Nathalie and the DEH staff threw me a surprise party that was attended by Americans, Germans, third country nationals, and many friends I had made over the years. There were more than 250 people at the party, which turned out to be a roast. I enjoyed it more than I can say.

Another wonderful memory that I carry is the day that Nathalie and I decided to have breakfast in Switzerland, lunch in France, and dinner in Germany. The boys were off attending a Boy Scout field trip and this was one of the nicest romantic getaways that I can recall.

When we left Germany, I came back to the states and accepted the assignment of Battalion Commander of the 92nd Engineer Construction Battalion at Fort Stewart, Georgia; the first African American to hold this position as well. This was a 600-man engineer combat battalion (heavy) that was equipped to execute combat and combat engineer missions on the battlefield or heavy construction in the garrison during peacetime. I'm proud to say that my battalion conducted the best marksmanship training and Nathalie and I had the best soldier family program in the brigade. While there, I established a Troop Construction Review Committee that assured more orderly and timely progress on projects and completed major projects worth $2.1 million that included new ranges for the M1 and M2 combat vehicles, a new motor pool, important domestic projects for local public schools, and the construction of a Boy Scout camp. I was privileged to serve under Major General Norman Schwarzkopf and he had this to say about my time there: *"In the short time he has been in command, his unit has accomplished all tasks and, in several cases, exceeded expectations. LTC Griffin is an aggressive, dynamic, enthusiastic commander who obviously enjoys what he is doing. He should be a strong contender for Senior Service College upon completion of his command tour."*

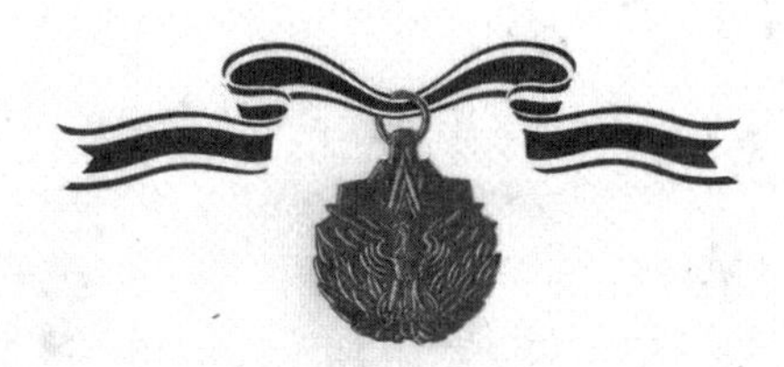

THE UNITED STATES OF AMERICA

TO ALL WHO SHALL SEE THESE PRESENTS, GREETING: THIS IS TO CERTIFY THAT THE PRESIDENT OF THE UNITED STATES OF AMERICA AUTHORIZED BY EXECUTIVE ORDER, 16 JANUARY 1969 HAS AWARDED

THE MERITORIOUS SERVICE MEDAL

(SECOND OAK LEAF CLUSTER)

TO LIEUTENANT COLONEL FLOYD LEE GRIFFIN, JR., UNITED STATES ARMY

FOR EXCEPTIONALLY MERITORIOUS SERVICE AS COMMANDER, 92D ENGINEER COMBAT BATTALION (HEAVY), 24TH INFANTRY DIVISION (MECHANIZED), FORT STEWART, GEORGIA FROM 2 JULY 1984 TO 2 JULY 1986. DURING LIEUTENANT COLONEL GRIFFIN'S COMMAND, THE BATTALION COMPLETED NINE MAJOR TROOP CONSTRUCTION PROJECTS AT THE HIGHEST ENGINEERING STANDARDS, THESE INCLUDED THE MODERNIZATION OF SEVERAL RANGES, NONCOMMISSIONED OFFICERS ACADEMY IMPROVEMENTS AND IMPORTANT DOMESTIC ACTION PROJECTS. HIS CONTRIBUTIONS TO THE VICTORY BRIGADE AND THE 24TH INFANTRY DIVISION WILL HAVE A LASTING EFFECT ON SOLDIERS AND THEIR FAMILIES FOR YEARS TO COME. HIS MERITORIOUS PERFORMANCE OF DUTY IS IN KEEPING WITH THE FINEST TRADITIONS OF MILITARY SERVICE AND REFLECTS GREAT CREDIT ON HIM, THIS COMMAND, AND THE UNITED STATES ARMY.

GIVEN UNDER MY HAND IN THE CITY OF WASHINGTON
THIS 12TH DAY OF JUNE 19 86

ANDREW L. COOLEY
MAJOR GENERAL, USA
COMMANDING

UNITED STATES OF AMERICA WAR OFFICE

SECRETARY OF THE ARMY

When I completed this assignment, I traveled to the Pentagon and served with the Office of the Assistant Chief of Engineers as a Military Construction Army Program Officer (Branch Chief) for one year. In this capacity, I reviewed and evaluated Military Construction Army (MCA) project documentation and interfaced with Army staff, the Army Secretariat, the Office of the Secretary of Defense, and Congress. I assisted in moving projects through the programming and budgeting process, defending these projects during budget reviews and Congressional hearings. I also assisted in assembling the Five-Year Defense Program and the President's Budget and served as a point of contact for NATO and Forces Command Construction Program.

Following this, I became the first African American to hold the position of Chief of the Engineer Officer Assignment Branch of the United States Total Army Personnel Agency, also in Washington DC. This was perhaps the most prestigious service that I had the honor to perform. Here, I supervised four assignment officers, one professional development officer, and four civilian employees in the management of the assignment and professional development of 4,900 Corps of Engineer officers. I recommended lieutenant colonels for battalion command and conducted career and professional development briefings worldwide for Engineer units and organizations. Considering the magnitude of this position, I can't help but be proud of my final rating by my superior officer, Colonel Thomas J. Hawes. *"LTC Griffin's performance has been outstanding. As the Engineer Branch Chief, he took charge of a branch whose credibility was lacking and whose assignment officers were crying for leadership. Floyd was quick to recognize the faults and moved quickly to set things right. The turnaround which has occurred is exceptional, a true monument to his dynamic leadership and managerial ability. LTC Griffin is totally responsive to his officers' needs, provides excellent command guidance and is looking ahead on how to expand his branch's operational ability. I could walk into his branch anytime and note the excellence in supervision, attention to detail, high morals, and a "can-do" attitude. He has molded his branch into a responsive "no nonsense" organization that has superb rapport with his proponent and is trusted by the officers in the field."*

Following these assignments with the Army Command & General Staff College, I attended the National War College in Washington DC., an institution that prepares future leaders of the Armed Forces, State Department, and other civilian agencies for high-level policy, command, and staff responsibilities. NWC conducts a senior-level course of study in national security policy and strategy for selected US and foreign military officers and federal officials. The same day that I graduated, I was promoted to full Colonel in the Pentagon by Major General Charles Williams, the same officer who promoted me to Lieutenant Colonel in Germany. My brother Toney came to my graduation and promotion ceremonies and I was on top of the world.

My last assignment was also in Washington, DC as Director of Contracts and Construction of the US Army Community Family Support Command. Once again, I was the first African American to hold this position. Here, I was responsible for planning, overseeing, and executing a $1 billion construction and contract budget world-wide and Army-wide. I was also responsible for defending the budget before Congress for appropriations and had about 250 people under me to carry out this position. I traveled extensively throughout the world to assure that the programs were being executed properly. After serving in this position for a year, I was selected to be the Command Engineer, a Senior Staff Officer, of the Southern Command in Panama, but I decided not to take this assignment because it was a two year non-accomplished assignment and Nathalie couldn't go with me. I decided to retire and we returned home to Milledgeville, Georgia.

I was fortunate to attend and graduate from one of the military's senior service institutions. This was the career path of every General officer in the Army, to include General Colin Powell and

Lieutenant General Russel L. Honore, two of the most famous Black Generals to attend one of the senior service institutions.

Black Colleges and the Military: Producers of Good Fruit

I started in the military in ROTC in 1962 and retired in 1990. I was able to achieve what I did largely because I was placed in learning environments and had the willingness to achieve. I learned from people who had gone to military academies and colleges and received major training assignments and significant educations. Our historical black colleges, like Tuskegee University, Howard University, Fort Valley State University, Hampton University, South Carolina State University and others around the country have provided the platform for us; providing the tools we need. These colleges produced capable black men and women who are able to compete in the world. It is amazing to reflect on how far we've come.

A Listing of My Major Military Assignments

- Graduated from Tuskegee Institute and commissioned 2nd Lieutenant
- 339th Engineer Battalion, Ft. Lewis, Washington. Construction Engineer Platoon Leader –
- Davison Army Airfield, Ft. Belvoir, Virginia. Rotary Wing Aviator - Flew VIP and senior officers around the DC area. Flew General William Westmoreland, Chairman, Joint Chief of Staff. Also commanded a training school company for 6 mos. Before leaving for Vietnam.
- 227th Assault Helicopter Battalion, IST Calvary Division, Vietnam. As a Battalion Intelligence Officer (S-2), and an instructor pilot.
- 93rd Engineer Construction Battalion, Commander Company A – in Vietnam. Responsible for major engineer maintenance of equipment. My company constructed roads; managed the sand and cement process to stabilize the soil for road construction.
- US Army, J. F. K. Center for Military Assistance, Ft Bragg, NC. Operations Staff Officer.
- US Army Institute for Military Affairs, Ft. Bragg, NC. Operation Training Officer, Brigade S-3 . Became president of the Interested Officers Association.
- Wake Forest University, /Winston-Salem State University, Winston-Salem, NC... the first African American to serve on the ROTC staff.
- 18th Engineer Brigade Construction, West Germany. Brigade Logistics Staff Officer (S-4)

- 79th Engineer Battalion Construction, West Germany Battalion Executive Officer
- U S Military Community, Karlsruhe, Germany... Director of Engineering and Housing, (First African American to hold this position)
- 92nd Engineer Battalion Construction, Ft. Steward, GA. Battalion Commander (First African American to command the battalion of 850 persons) 1984.
- Office of Assistant Chief of Engineers, Pentagon, Washington DC. Branch Chief Construction Programming Div., US Army Staff.
- US Army Total Army Personnel Command, Washington DC. Chief Engineer Officers Assignment Branch (First African American to hold this prestigious position; responsible for the development of 5,000 Corps of Engineer officers' professional development., etc. Branch Chief is a Lt. Colonel Position.
- US Army Community Family Support Center, Washington DC. Director Contracts and Construction. Oversaw the Army's construction of most building, materials on all bases throughout the world. Would travel around the world managing project. First African American at this post.

Awards And Decorations

- Legion of Merit (1)
- Bronze Star Medal (3)
- Meritorious Service Award (5)
- Air Medal (5)
- Army Commendation Medal (2)
- Army Achievement Medal (1)
- National Defense Service Medal (1)
- Vietnam Service Medal (1)

- Army Service Ribbon (1)
- Vietnam Commendation Medal (1)
- Republic of Vietnam Service Commendation Medal

Badges

- Army Aviator Badge
- Parachute Badge

Major Schools And Colleges

- National War College
- Command and General Staff College
- Engineer Officers Advance School
- Engineer Officers Basic School
- Rotary Wing Aviator School
- Instructor Pilot (OH-6) School
- Airborne School

Civilian Education

- M.S. Florida Institute of Technology.
- B.A. Tuskegee Institute
- A.D. Gupton- Jones Funeral Service

Speeches Addresses and Note

Farewell Address to the Interested Officers Association

Mr. President-elect, elected officers, special guests and brother officers of the Interested Officers Association (IOA), tonight is both a happy and sad occasion for me. It is a happy occasion because the IOA is continuing its interest and concern for community development and professional development of the Officers Corps, especially the minority officers, the basis upon which this organization was founded. Likewise, it is a sad occasion for me because it marks the end of my involvement with the IOA, since I will be departing Fort Bragg to attend the Engineer Advance Course at Fort Belvoir, Virginia, in mid-July. So, this is my farewell address to you.

I would like to thank the officers who have served with me during the past 12 months for their untiring dedication to the IOA and to our various projects and goals. And [I give thanks] to the members of the IOA for their continued support and confidence in me as your president. I have done the best I know how as your president, the very best I could. I have served you, and shall continue to the very end to serve you, to the best of my ability. This organization must continue to be the very best. This organization must continue to strive to be a dynamic organization in the Fort Bragg/ Fayetteville communities. You must continue to have pride in the purpose for which this organization was founded. You must continue to improve the professional and personal qualities of the association's membership through participation in military and civilian education programs, the encouragement of job expertise, and the development of strong leadership traits. Yes, you must continue, not only continue to have pride and be a dynamic organization, but you must help to develop the kinds of officers the U.S. Army needs so badly to give our young soldiers a sense of pride in being a part of the best Army in the world.

The glory of our past and the dignity of our present must lead the way for our young soldiers and the only way this can be accomplished is through good leadership. I am convinced that the IOA is an organization that can accomplish this task. In closing, I would like to end with a statement made by one of our great generals, a statement that is very close to me as a professional soldier in the United States Army: "Duty. Honor. Country. Those three hallowed words reverently dictate what you ought to be, what you can be, what you will be. They are your rallying points: to build courage when courage seems to fail; to regain faith when there seems to be little cause for faith; to create hope when hope becomes forlorn." And I would like for you to remember: There is no mission too difficult; there is no task too great; duty first. Good luck and I will always be a part of the IOA.

♦♦♦♦♦♦♦♦♦♦♦♦♦♦♦♦♦♦♦♦♦♦

History of the Interested Officers Association

In the spring of 1971, several young Army officers at Fort Bragg came together in an effort to find ways and means of supplementing existing entertainment activities in order to add more relevance and variety to their social lives. Throughout the spring and summer of '71 these officers used their ingenuity and creativity to plan many unique and successful group oriented social activities to primarily benefit the Black community. The year's climax was the staging of the most talked about formal affair in recent Fayetteville history — The Interested Officers Association Yuletide Ball which brought together hundreds of grass root and professional military and civilian people in the Fayetteville-Fort Bragg community.

The primary purpose of the event was to help bring people together at Christmas-time. The organization decided that it was most fitting and proper to donate the proceeds from the function to an organization that was either doing research on a cure for Sickle Cell Anemia or one that was conducting a screening and testing program to identify and assist people with Sickle Cell or the trait. The Duke University Sickle Cell Fund, which is composed of several Black medical students at Duke was the recipient of the "IOA's" initial contribution. These students were conducting a screening and testing program.

The "IOA" has sponsored several other military-civilian gatherings. On Armed Forces Day the organization sponsored a special education class from a local elementary school at Fort Bragg's Annual festivities. The students enthusiastically took advantage of the opportunity to observe and play "GI Joe" with much of the military equipment on display.

In early July the Interested Officers Association sponsored a very successful gathering of minority ROTC cadets at the Officers Club to help acclimate them to military life. At the event the cadets had the opportunity to communicate with fellow cadets from all area colleges, Junior and field grade officers, and yes, even Generals. The event was quite meaningful to the cadets as well as the officers. The organization is continuing to assist the cadets in other worthwhile programs while they are in summer camp.

The Interested Officers Association will continue to strive to be a meaningful force in rendering assistance to the civilian and military community in areas where there is a need.

The Interested Officers Association

Members of the Interested Officers Assn. Ft. Bragg, NC, 1972. Captain Floyd L. Griffin, Jr, President.

OFFICERS

President .... **FLOYD L. GRIFFIN (CPT)**
Vice-President . **EDWARD M. ANDERSON (CPT)**
Secretary .. **SAMUEL A. McFARLAND III (CPT)**
Treasurer .... **MATTHEW R. BOWMAN (LT)**
Trustee .... **DONALD L. FEREBEE (CPT)**

MEMBERS

Gorham L. Black III (Maj)
George G. Franklin, Jr. (Maj)
Louis L. Craven (Cpt)
Ozzie Corbin, Jr. (Cpt)
Carlton G. Epps (Cpt)
Stephen M. Feigenbaum (Cpt)
Gene A. King (Cpt)
Reginald T. Lewis (Cpt)
Joseph H. Lofton (Cpt)
Calvin B. Wimbish (Lt)
Anthony R. Morehead (Cpt)
Theodore W. Nell (Cpt)
Willie Pitts, Jr. (Cpt)
John J. Qatsha (Cpt)
David L. Ridgell (Cpt)
Larry M. Spence (Cpt)
Gilliam P. Nelson (1Lt)
Chester Garrett III (Maj)
Hillard L. Holland, Jr. (Cpt)
John M. Brown (Lt)
Ernest L. Jones, Jr. (Lt)
Alphonso W. Knight, Jr. (Lt)
William E. Ward (Lt)
Oveta Whaley (Lt)
George W. Barnes (CW4)
Robert B. Clark, (CW2)
Lloyd S. Diliard (CW2)
Olanda Gore (CW2)
Campbell E. Sherman (Cpt)

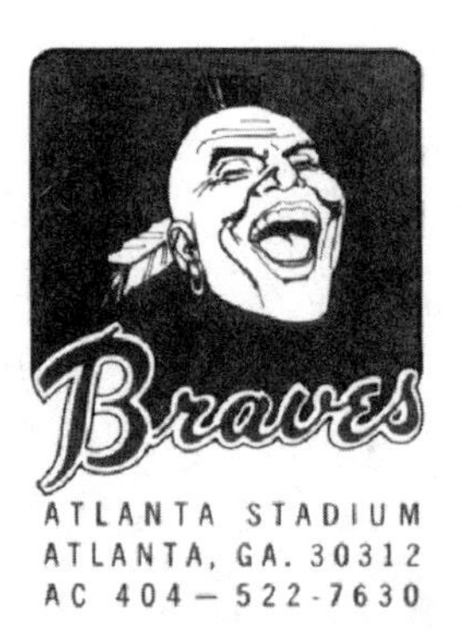

ATLANTA STADIUM
ATLANTA, GA. 30312
AC 404 — 522-7630

July 31, 1972

Captain Floyd L. Griffin
President
Interested Officers Association
P. O. Box 62
Fort Bragg, North Carolina 28307

Dear Captain Griffin:

As the Braves will be playing in Montreal on August 18, it will be impossible for me to attend your benefit for the war against sickle cell anemia.

I do want to thank you for the kind invitation, and I am sure your festivities that evening will be a tremendous success.

With kindest regards, I am

Sincerely,

Hank Aaron

Hank Aaron

HA/ck

Senator Griffin's
FAMILY REUNION SPEECH

THEME: "EMBRACING OUR FUTURE"
TOPIC: "TAKING CONTROL OF OUR DESTINY"

Good afternoon family. You look young, vibrant, strong, and happy. That's a sign that you have been eating well! God has truly blessed you to be a wonderful family. Through fate and pleasure, you have stuck together. And I think that you should give yourself a hand for that.

The African American family has come a long way in the united states of America since the first slave ship landed here. We have endured a lot. We have won and we have lost. Laws were passed so that we could be recognized as human beings. We have marched, bled, died, and lived to fight again, just to defend our humanity.

We live better and earn more than we ever have before at any period in human history since we first toiled the soils of this country. Yet, all is not well for African Americans in this country. We are now facing new and more threatening circumstances today. It is an understatement to say that much of the African American family and community are on the verge of extinction statistically and visually and it is a woeful drama that is being lived out daily upon the stage of every home, village, and metropolis in America. Sociologically, all the statistics would have us dead, embalmed, and ready for viewing.

Some of the data that I have reviewed presents some realistic and hard assumed facts about us. We make up 13% of America's population, but 50% of all those arrested for murder are African Americans, as are 41 percent of the victims; the leading cause of death for African American men between the ages of 16 and 34, murder. 35% of African American men live in urban populations are drug or alcohol abusers; 46% of African American males ages 16-62 are unemployed; 32% earn less than the poverty level; 30% of all African American families live below the poverty level; the African American infant mortality rate is 50% higher than that of whites and 89% of all births by African American teenagers are illegitimate! These are depressing statistics and they reveal that our situation requires immediate attention. We cannot ignore these spine chilling statistics.

How did things become so bad and brutal for such a promising and potential filled people? Where did the train jump the track? Where did we throw the cargo overboard? I suggest that the following are possible reasons for our disarray:

1. *Slavery - at the root of our problem is the historical fact of slavery and its continuing legacy of self-hatred, divisiveness, and hostility at the male/female level.*
2. *The collective assault of racism - personal racism is not a major concern for African Americans. The major concern is institutional racism where African Americans are guaranteed to have a second class orientation.*
3. *The pseudo premise of integration - we believed that what the white man had was better. We naively believed that if we could just sit next to white people, there would be a great social transformation. Integration has done more to hurt us than to help us.*
4. *The drug culture - drugs have become an economic medium for much of our community.*
5. *The 'Vietnam war - this war gave birth to an attitude of cynicism and despair in regards to those in positions of authority.*
6. *The disappearance of the structures of discipline such as: the community, the church, and the school.*
7. *Parental delinquency - this leads to juvenile delinquency. Parents in many instances gave up on trying to guide their children, and instead became partners in permissiveness.*
8. *A sexual ethic of exploitation - this leads to "babies having babies".*

These are possible reasons for the cloud that hangs and hovers above our heads. Yet, I maintain that we can still `take control of our destiny' in this country. I do not profess to have the answers, but I can offer some suggestions.

The first thing that I invite us to understand is that the 'family' is important. God created the first family according to the Judeo-Christian teaching:

> *"And the Lord God formed man of the dust of life; and man became a living soul… And the Lord God caused a deep sleep to fall upon Adam… And he took one of his ribs… And made a woman."*

God took the initiative to create Adam and Eve. Love was at the center of God's movement towards structuring the family. Adam and Eve were created to be partners and not foes. God reminded them that they were not God.

WHAT DO WE LEARN FROM THE FIRST FAMILY MODEL?

1. *The family is divinely formulated.*
2. *Man cannot live successfully outside of God.*
3. *The family is to be built upon a divine-human partnership.*
4. *The family is strong when we are in agreement with God.*
5. *There is no superior/inferior relationship. It is complimentary.*

We must love and nurture our family and family members. We must return to helping and holding each other. We must renew our trust and forgiveness of one another. We must fight for each other. If we just do some of these things, then we will see a significant change in our families.

My second suggestion is that we end the male/female hostility that haunts and hurts us. We must recognize that there is a 'terrible hostility between African American males and females.

Often the white male power structure pits the African American female against the African American male. In the job market, an African American female is frequently hired first and advanced ahead of an African American male, thereby creating undue jealousy and misunderstanding. Instead of falling into that trap and focusing on our differences, males and females need to join together and gain strength from our similarities.

1. *Parents must teach their children the virtues of love and respect.*
2. *Parents must become educated in the psychological art of aggression on the African American family in order to break the cycle of hostility.*

3. *Parents must teach their children what it means to be an African American in a racist society.*
4. *Parents must teach their children the responsibilities of marriage and parenthood.*
5. *Parents must teach their young male children how to love an African American female and teach their young female children how to love an African American male. There is no more room in our community for premarital sex and irresponsible baby- making.*
6. *In any relationship, males and females must treat each other with dignity and respect.*
7. *Since both are victims of oppression, they must become comrades in liberation.*
8. *Parents should begin this training when their children are between the ages of 3-5 years old.*

Men and women --we are on the same team! We are fighting in the same war for the same purpose and we need each other.

My final suggestion is that we instill values in our children. They live in a different time and world than we grew up in. But I am here to tell you that in any world - right is right and wrong is wrong. In any world, respect is respect and disrespect is disrespect. I agree that some things may appear to be old fashioned, but they got us where we are today.

Somehow, we must instill decency and respect into our children at an early age. We must teach them to say yes ma'am and no ma'am: yes sir and no sir, we must not tolerate "naw' and "yeah".

We must work to encourage our children to finish school and not drop out. They must see and understand the necessity of a quality education. They must understand that if they cannot read, write, and communicate effectively, then their choices will be poor in life.

We must teach our children to respect females. They must reject the labels that gangsta rap places upon females. Nobody's daughter is the five letter word that begins with "b" or the other five letter word that begins with "w". Females are to be loved and adored.

We must teach our children to love God and go to church. There is no substitute for God. God is their guide through life. To live life outside of God is both tragic and terrible. To live life inside God is prosperous and peaceful.

Yes, the African American family is under siege. But we can control much of our destiny. We have the intelligence, spirituality, resources, and ability to turn this ship around. All is not lost. We simply must fight harder. If we want a brighter future, then we must fight harder. If we want to prosper in the future, then we, must fight' harder. If we want to grow into the next millennium, then we must fight harder. Keep the family alive. Don't you give up. We have come too far and gained too much.

I charge you with the old Negro spiritual:

"Guide me, 0 thou great Jehovah, pilgrim through this barren land; I am weak, but thou art mighty - hold me with thy powerful hand: bread of heaven, bread of heaven, feed me till I want no more, feed me till I want no more."

With God guiding us, we can make it

Self Motivation

Some people seem to attract success, wealth, attainment, recognition and personal satisfaction, apparently with very little effort. Others reach these goals with the greatest difficulty, while still others never seem to reach them at all. What is the difference? It can't be physical and it's a proven fact that such ability is not inherited. Obviously then, the power, the capacity to achieve outstanding success must come from within the people themselves. It's this same quality that you possess, to a greater or lesser degree, in yourself, and if you want to change your wishes into fact, your dreams into reality, your desires into solid achievements, the all-important answer is personal motivation. Personal motivation is exactly what those two words indicate: the ability to motivate yourself to accomplish. Personal motivation means the development of inner strength, conscious willpower, overwhelming desire, and the personal determination to reach any goal you want to achieve. It doesn't matter who you are, or what your age might be, if you want to achieve personal sustaining success, the motivation to drive you toward that goal must come from within. It must be personal, deep-rooted and a part of your innermost thoughts. Personal motivation is based on the scientific principle that each of us is the end result of what we think.

Strange Fruit

Even good parents like the Army and an HBCU (Historically Black College and University) can produce children who have quirks and peculiarities. That would be me. Despite the strict dress code enforced by the military—or perhaps, on some unconscious level, *because* of it—I began wearing cowboy boots while stationed in Germany. I would wear them when I wore civilian clothing, even formal wear. After leaving the Army, I continued to wear boots, and purchased more of them. Over time, people began inquiring about them whenever I didn't have them on. The boots have developed into a signature, of sorts, these days.

Another fondness I have is cigars. Whenever one of my soldiers' wives had a baby, they would give me a cigar. I did not smoke them often, but I always had an unlit one in my mouth. I was content just chewing on it—until something was troubling me or I was about to "go off" on someone. Only then would I light it. Among my soldiers and colleagues, the word got out that when Major Griffin lit his cigar, you knew he was mad. For years, no matter where I was stationed in the Army, that reputation about the cigar followed me. A reputation for both—the cigar chewing and the boot wearing—has followed me since.

"Major Smoke" Floyd L. Griffin, XO, 79th Engineering Battalion, Germany

Rise Up Black Men

(Speech delivered by Senator Griffin)

We have been blessed to live to see the 21st Century. None of us had any idea that we would be here on this day in this century. As the grown folk used to say when I was growing up, "The Lord has allowed our golden moments to roll on a little while longer."

We are living in an exciting time. Our opportunities and possibilities are unlimited. For black people in America, our journey has been up and down. To quote the hymn writer, "We have come through many dangers, toils and snares."

While this country has experienced unprecedented economic growth, black people are still not getting all that we should. As we move further into his new century, black men are going to have to step back up to the plate. We have a long history of black men who have marched, fought, bled and died to get us to this point. Men like Adam Clayton Powell, Jr., the famous preacher and congressman from Harlem; Dr. Martin Luther King, Jr. who marched and never fired one bullet; Malcolm X who was misunderstood; Nat Turner who led a slave revolt; Fredrick Douglas who published his own paper; Dr. Charles Drew who discovered blood plasma; and the list goes on.

But where are the Black Men today? There is too much pain and suffering in our communities. There is a void and a giant gap in leadership in our community. The Black Man was a once feared social giant, but now too few people take us seriously! One-fourth of black men are in jail, one-fourth are on parole and another fourth are just hanging. As a result, you have just one-fourth who are trying to lead and lift up our race.

The sleeping giant must awaken from his sleep and reassume his role. Too many black women are carrying the full load. Too many children are assuming the head-of-household role. Too many teenagers are calling the shots. Why? Because the black male giant has fallen asleep!

Black Men, your families are calling you to wake up.

Black Men, your children are calling you to wake up.

Black men, our communities are calling you to wake up.

Black men, your churches are calling you to wake up.

More importantly, God is calling you to stand up!

God has always worked through black men to lead his people. Moses was a black Hebrew who led the liberation movement in Egypt. King Solomon was a black king and the son of King David who built the temple after David died. Martin Luther King, Jr. . . . you know the story. Black Men, you have a rich and royal heritage. You are direct descendents of the great Kings and Queens of Africa. You have to wake up and be the men that God has called you to be!

I would like to suggest three areas in which we as Black Men need to wake up:

First, we must awaken and define our priorities. Black men must decide what should be first. Black men must make God the center of their lives. Life begins and ends with God. He is the head of our lives. All that we have and hope to be begins in God. When we put God first, then the rest of our lives will fall into place. Problems are easier to solve with God on your side. Mountains are easier to climb with God on your side. Black Men, make God your first priority.

Our second priority should be family. Black Men take charge of your family. Too many of us are so busy outside of the home that we do not spend enough time inside the home. Make your wife and children a priority. If every black man spent 15 more minutes per day with his children, he would see major improvements in their lives. The strength of any community rests in strong families. Black Men, your families need you. Make your family a priority by providing for them. God has said that you are the head of the household. Act like you are the head. Walk like you are the head. Live and lead like you are the head. Abraham was a family man. Joshua was a family man. Peter was a family man.

Black Men must make community involvement a priority. I challenge every black man here today to become involved in their community. Get involved in your community and fight for good representation on the school board, county commission, city council, in the court house and in the state house.

The third way that black men can stand up is to engage in possibility thinking. We must expand our minds beyond doing just enough to get by. We must expand our minds beyond blending into the crowd. We must expand our minds beyond going along to get along. We must expand our minds beyond the "this is all we deserve attitude."

Black Men need to think big. Why can't you have more? Why can't you win an election? Why can't you make more money? The bible teaches us that as a man thinks in his heart, so he is. If we think little, then we will live little. If we expand our thinking, then we will expand the way that we live. Black men must think bigger as we move further into this new century. You must think about setting and reaching goals. You must think about economic development. You must think about politics. You must think about education. You must think about race relations. You must think about securing a better future for your families. You must think about technology and the need to close the digital divide. If we do not learn more about computers real fast, we will be left behind.

Much of the success you hope to aspire to begins with thinking. You must paint a mental picture of what you want to do and then do it! We must teach our children to think. Possibility thinking will be one of their tickets through life. Moses thought about freeing the Jews. Joshua thought about marching around Jericho. Nat Turner thought about a slave revolt.

Finally Black Men, I challenge you to stand up in the area of progress. We cannot rest on the laurels of the past. We cannot continue to brag and boast about where we have been. We have not made it!

While we make more money than we have ever made, Whites still make more money than Blacks. While we have larger homes, Blacks are still turned down for loans at two times the rate of Whites. While we have better jobs, Whites are still two times as likely to have a management position. While we have black elected officials in Georgia, and we have recently had a couple of black governors and senators elected into office, we still do not have a black governor. While our population is growing, Hispanics will replace us as the largest American minority in the next 20 years. We have not arrived. We have made progress, but we must make more progress! Racial injustice is still alive! It is alive in the fight to destroy Affirmative Action. It is alive in the fight to wipe out majority African American Congressional and Legislative Districts. It is alive in job discrimination. It is alive in lending practices. It is alive in Corporate America and it is alive here in Mobile politics.

Black Men, you must wake up and make more progress. We must be like the mythical phoenix and rise up out of the ashes and soar to new heights. We have our heads in the sand like the proverbial ostrich, and unless we get it out of the sand, we will fall even farther behind.

Making progress is fighting for what you believe in. Making progress is finding a cause and seeing it through until the end. Making progress is voting in elections. Making progress is building up your community. Making progress is mentoring black boys. Making progress is taking charge of your own destiny and not waiting on a piece of legislation to make it happen.

Life does not owe you anything Black Man. It is up to you to pick up the pen of creativity and write our own story. Write that story so well that the world will have to beat a path to your door and ask you, "How did you do it?" This new millennium is filled with numerous possibilities. We are living in some exciting times, but if we are going to be successful, we must: 1) Define our priorities, 2) engage in possibility thinking, and 3) make progress.

Black Men, I challenge you to rise up in the spirit of your "ancestors".

Black Men, I challenge you to rise up in the spirit of "progress".

Black Men, I challenge you to rise up in the spirit of "new possibilities".

Black Men, I charge you to rise up in the spirit of "reason and reality".

Black Men, I challenge you to rise up in the spirit of "courage".

Black Men, I challenge you to rise up and mentor black boys and rise up over the power of the enemy.

When you rise up Black Men, your proverbial Red Sea will part. When you rise up Black Men, your Jericho Walls will come tumbling down. When you rise up Black Men, your midnight will turn into day!

Rise up Black Men and return to being the men that God has created and called you to be!

Black History Month Message
By Senator Floyd Griffin

We are in the midst of Black History month. When we look back over our history, we can be very proud of what we have accomplished as Black people in America. When you consider that we were brought to this country against our will and we have overcome slavery, segregation, poll taxes and a host of other horrible injustices, we have a lot to celebrate.

Our journey has been both rich and rough. It has been both troublesome and triumphant. It has been both a blessing and a burden. Yet, we have managed to keep our heads up. Our faith in almighty God has been a guiding force in our pursuit of the American Dream. What is the American Dream? The answer depends on who you are asking and what their nightmare is. For African Americans, the American Dream is no different than any other Americans. The dream is the desire to be treated equally, the right to pursue a job, the right to feed our families, the right to educate our children, and the right to have our seat at the table of justice.

We have won our freedom from slavery which was no easy task. We have overcome segregation which was no easy task. We have overcome the poll tax in order to vote which was no easy task and too many of us still won't vote! We have scored victories with Affirmative Action which was no easy task. Yet, there is still another tier to the Civil Rights Movement and that is our "Silver Rights" which is economic freedom. The importance of African American businesses is now more important than ever.

There is so much debate and discussion about the new millennium. In my opinion as far as African American people are concerned, the number one issue for us in the 21st Century will be "Silver Rights". If we are to be successful, not only must we have money, we must use it wisely. Dr. Martin Luther King, Jr. said:

"The economic highway to power has few entry lanes for Negroes. Nothing so vividly reveals the crushing impact of discrimination and the heritage of exclusion as the limited dimensions for Negro business in the most powerful economy in the world."

Therefore, if we are to be victorious on the social scene in America, we must develop a healthy attitude about wealth and Black businesses. Black businesses are vital to the black community. We must do a better job of supporting our own businesses. Likewise, black businesses must also provide us with quality services. Black people in America generate $200 billion dollars. Yet, we spend very little of that with black businesses. In fact, our money only stays in the black community about four hours. We must get our people to understand and believe that our ice is just as cold as the other people's. We must quit penalizing each other because we are Black. We have developed a mentality that Asians are better business people than we are. There was a time that black businesses lined both sides of the street. Now we have to look far and hard to find successful black businesses. We must take care of our own. We must return to an interdependent community where what happens to you affects me. Remember when you were short on sugar and you could go next door and borrow some? We need to get back to doing that. Either all of us fail or all of succeed.

There are enough Black people to support every black business in this community and every community across this land. Black businesses also have a role to play. We who own a black business must become involved in the community. Our voices must provide leadership and focus. We cannot just sell and provide services; we must also be visible in the churches and schools. We have a vital role to play in the community and people look to us for leadership. People have a fundamental respect for us and expect us to steer them in the right direction. The black pastor and the black funeral home owner are two of the most influential people in any Black community that you enter. We must support community programs and ideas that will advance the cause and efforts of the community. There is nothing wrong with black business owners setting up scholarships for needy students or being mentors for our children. What is wrong with donating time and talent to worthy community causes that will make a difference in the lives of those with whom we do business?

We must not just sell, but we must also serve. We must not just beg, but also bless. We must not jut get, but we must also give. Life is never measured by how much we get, but how much we give. Give to the community as often as you can within your limits.

Finally, black businesses must also become more involved in the political process. Most things that we do in this life revolved around and are affected by politics. Politics determine how much you are going to pay, when you are going to pay, and will let you know what will happen when you fail to pay. Black business owners must become politically astute or continue to get left out of the "political game". For some reason we are trapped into the thought that "they" are going to do what they want, regardless of what we say or do. We must change our attitude in this area and begin to step up and stand out in the political arena. People only have a much power as we give them.

Jesse Jackson said earlier this month in Atlanta, "Our challenge is to do something that we think that we cannot do and that is to out think white people." He went on to say, "They cannot be as smart as we think they are and do as many dumb things as they do." Our vote and voice do count in the political system. Georgia elected a new Governor because we had the highest African American turnout in the nation during the 1998 election. We elected the first African American Labor Commissioner because of the Black vote in 1998. We elected the only African American Attorney General in the Untied States of America because of the Black vote in 1998. We could have elected a Black to the second highest position in the state, but we did not. Why? We count and we will continue to count. We must never resign ourselves to thinking that we do not have political power. Black business owners must master the art of local politics because this is where we can make the truest difference. Most politics are local in some sense.

Black business owners must support and push candidates that will push an agenda that is advantageous to the African American community. We must also hold our candidates accountable once we elected them. We should constantly remind them that they were elected to put our needs first and foremost on the agenda. We must let them know that they are not there to sell us out, but to help us get on a level playing field. Black politicians should always be sensitive to our needs. While there are some good white politicians, we cannot assume that they are going to let the bread of prosperity fall on our table. A rising tide usually raises all boats, but we have discovered that the American tide is prejudiced. Usually the white boats are lifted while our boats are left to flounder in the shallow waters of defeatism.

Not only must we participate in the political system, we must understand how it works. Politics creates wealth and we deserve our fair share of the economic pie. We have everything that we fought for but none of what we need. We fought to end slavery, but we need security. We fought to end segregation, but we need success. We fought to get the right to vote, but we need a voice. Politics is one means to some of the ends that we need to meet. Black business people, you have the power to make a difference. We have stood on the shoulders of other and now it is time for us to allow others to stand on our shoulders. We must learn the art of transmitting wealth. Too often it is true that the first generation creates the wealth, the second generation spends it, and the third generation goes on welfare. That must stop! We must develop and maintain a healthy attitude toward work. We must work diligently to instill in young boys and girls the importance of working for ourselves in order to build a strong people. We must begin to view each African American family as a business corporation. We must learn individually and collectively how to budget our monies and live within our means. We cannot buy limousines when we don't have cab fare. We must become producers rather than just consumers. To quote Rev. Joseph Lowery, "Much of our destinies are in our own hands. Nobody owes us anything. We owe life. Therefore, pick up the pen of creativity and write your own story so well that our children want to be like us and do more, and have more, and give more.

Let's get to work and build bigger and stronger black businesses that will serve not just our community, but all communities. We always talk about wanting to be the best and have the best. My advice to us is what John Madden said about John Elway of the Denver Broncos, "If you want to be the greatest, you must strive for perfection."

THE UNITED STATES OF AMERICA

TO ALL WHO SHALL SEE THESE PRESENTS, GREETING: THIS IS TO CERTIFY THAT THE PRESIDENT OF THE UNITED STATES OF AMERICA AUTHORIZED BY ACT OF CONGRESS 20 JULY 1942 HAS AWARDED

THE LEGION OF MERIT

TO COLONEL FLOYD L. GRIFFIN, JR., CORPS OF ENGINEERS
UNITED STATES ARMY

FOR exceptionally meritorious conduct in the performance of outstanding service from July 1980 thru July 1990 while assigned in a variety of positions, most recently as Director, Construction and Contracts, United States Army Community and Family Support Center. His exemplary leadership, dedication, professionalism and personal commitment to excellence have resulted in significant and lasting contributions to the readiness and well being of the Army. Colonel Griffin's outstanding service and distinctive achievements over a twenty year career are in keeping with the finest traditions of military service and reflect great credit on him and the United States Army.

GIVEN UNDER MY HAND IN THE CITY OF WASHINGTON
THIS 9TH DAY OF APRIL 19 90

William Gilsichan II
THE ADJUTANT GENERAL

M. P. W. Stone
SECRETARY OF THE ARMY

Part II

Civilian Life, Politics and a New Era of Leadership

Floyd L. Griffin, Jr.

Chapter 6

Coming Home

After 23 years and 14 assignments in different parts of the world, where I carted my family around so that we could, indeed, be a family, I decided it was time to retire from active duty. My sons, Brian and Eric, had attended U.S. military-sponsored schools throughout their school careers and had received excellent education because of it. Nathalie and I looked forward to being closer to our families, as our parents were getting older. We had each faced the crisis of the passing of loved ones while we lived and were stationed abroad and we felt that it was time to be closer to our roots. In keeping with this, we felt the need for Brian and Eric to attend HBCU's, and particularly to consider Tuskegee University as a choice in furthering their education. Our desires, and our sons' self-determined decisions, paid off. Today, Eric is a senior technical strategy advisor for Microsoft.

"My Dad has inspired me, as a son, to work hard, the way he has all his life," said Eric. "His favorite expression is "Winners make it happen." He never explained what the phrase meant, but he demonstrated it by example. From his military, political and business careers, he has made things happen by succeeding despite setbacks, obstacles and naysayers. As a father, he has been a steady supporting influence in my life as I have faced life's challenges. He has always been ready to give measured advice without telling me what to do. He has always been sure to let me know that he was there for me, no matter what happened. The most important values I have learned about my

father came not because of his successes but because of his failures. He has not succeeded at everything, but each time he fell down, he picked himself up to rise and achieve higher goals."

"I have used my father's example in my own career where I have worked for Fortune 500 companies like Apple Computer and Microsoft."

"I can only hope to pass on such values to my sons."

Our son, Lieutenant Colonel Brian E. Griffin is a career Army officer serving as a Plans Officer in the Department of the Army, Assistant Chief of Staff Installation Management at the Pentagon, in Washington, DC. Brian shares his thoughts for which I am grateful.

"Thanks to my dad, I am the man, the father, and the officer that I am today. This is because I saw my dad as my role model while growing up. Dad has always been there for Eric and me, especially in a time when young African American men needed to have a man in their lives. If I had to describe dad in a sentence, I would say that he is a man who can make a decision, a man who is dependable, a man who always looks out for the best interests of his loved ones, a man who does the right thing, even if it is not popular. These are all attributes that dad instilled in both Eric and me."

"Probably the most valuable life lessons that my parents taught us was the importance of education, how to face challenges and to look for opportunities to make a difference. Our parents always stressed the importance of academics. You could say that was basically our job as children in the Griffin household. We were not allowed to watch TV or go outside until our homework was completed. As a child, I thought that was unfair, however our parents always had our best interest in mind. Their beliefs and standards did not only apply to us. I remember the long hours of studying that dad did when we lived in Melbourne, Florida in the mid-1970's when dad earned his master's degree at Florida Institute of Technology. From observing dad's commitment to improve himself, I learned early to work hard to stay competitive so when the time came for college, numerous educational choices were open to me."

"Another memory was when we were stationed in Winston-Salem, North Carolina and Dad was an Army's Reserve Officers Training Corps (ROTC) Instructor

at both Wake Forest University and Winston-Salem State University. This assignment gave him an opportunity to represent the Army at both of these universities to tell the Army story. On numerous occasions, Dad would take Eric and me to work with him where we were able to observe how he interacted with his students. The respect given to him by faculty and students made me feel special, and gave me the belief that I could make a difference in someone else's life as well."

"Following my father's advice, I decided to enroll in the Army's Reserve Officers Training Corps (ROTC) program at Tuskegee (Institute) University, and I graduated in 1989 with a degree in Architecture. I believe that I fulfilled a portion of my parent's dreams when they pinned on my gold bars making me an officer that same year."

"Even today, our parents continue to be actively involved in our families' lives. They take time out every summer to bring their grandchildren to Milledgeville to participate in local educational activities and events to help them get ahead in life."

Nathalie and I had longed for the time when I could come home and not have to announce, "We've been moved." Our final move was to Milledgeville, a place in which I had not resided for 28 years. I had visited, of course—we had brought the boys back regularly to visit their grandparents, with whom they had wonderfully bonded. But *residing* in Milledgeville was not the same as visiting. My new challenge would involve finding a comfortable role in the small-town setting and using the leadership, management and organization skills I had learned over the years to assist in growing Slater's Funeral Home, the family business. To that end, I enrolled in Gupton-Jones College, a funeral-service school, to become a funeral director and embalmer. My sister Delbra and with my parents were doing an excellent job of running the business when I returned, but I wanted to contribute to their efforts, and I wanted to do it properly. Hence, as I had done throughout my military career, I approached the new challenge by arming myself with formal education.

THE IDEA TO ENTER INTO POLITICS

As I settled in beyond the allure of "hometown boy comes home," the agendas and objectives of people in local and regional politics really began to ring clear to me. My background in organizational management, structure, leadership and responsibility called into question the motives of some of the people in public office. As a retired Army Colonel whose last assignment was at the Pentagon, I continued working in the family business improving our service to the community but with a view toward a new challenge. I had not run for a political office before. Baldwin County was a good 'test kitchen' for how accepting a majority White population would accept a viable Black candidate for public office in middle Georgia in 1993.

A political campaign is a strategic nightmare of planning, positioning, fundraising and appearances. It calls for a candidate to put in long hours and a series of real roll-up-your-sleeves and get-the-word-out type challenges. Things like making phone calls daily to enlist financial support, volunteers and votes are common activities.

I ran and lost my first race for a seat on the Baldwin County Commission. I learned a lot in a short period about local and state level politics. The name recognition among people in the county and the media was priceless. I met a number of community leaders, politicians and even the Governor of the State of Georgia, Zell Miller. I met lobbyists, political strategists, and numerous members of the house and the senate. My interest in possibly of running for state senate was peaked as a result of some unsavory comments made by an ungrateful incumbent, Senator Wilbur Baugh. Even before I met him I'd witnessed how unconcerned he was. The taxpayers deserved better representation than someone who would take his constituents for granted. The governor wasn't pleased with his attendance or his voting record. After mapping out a strategy and conducting a good straw poll to determine how much support I would have, I filed to enter the campaign. My team was assembled and I entered the race for state senate. It would be a three candidate race; Senator Baugh, Marty Fierman, an Eatonton attorney and myself. Leon Mitchell, a dear friend, agreed to become my campaign manager.

Winners and Losers

A winner says, "Let's found out"; a loser says, "Nobody knows."

A winner knows what to fight for and knows when to compromise; a loser compromises on what he shouldn't and fights for what isn't worthwhile.

A winner shows he's sorry by making up for what he's done; a loser says, "I'm sorry," but does the same thing the next time.

A winner says, "There ought to be a better way to do it"; a loser says, "That's the way it's always been done here."

A winner makes every concession he can, short of sacrificing his basic principles; a loser is so afraid of making concessions that he hangs onto pride while his principles go down the drain.

A winner, in the end, gives more than he takes; a loser dies clinging to the illusion that "winning" means taking more than you give.

A winner listens; a loser just waits until it's his turn to talk.

A winner respects those who are superior to him and tries to learn something from them; a loser resents those who are superior to him and tries to find chinks in their armor.

A winner is not afraid to contradict himself when faced with a contradictory situation; a loser is more concerned with being consistent than with being right.

A winner knows that people will be kind if you give them the chance; a loser feels that people will be unkind if you give them the chance.

A winner takes a big problem and separates it into smaller parts so that it can be more easily manipulated; a loser takes a lot of little problems and rolls them together until they are unsolvable.

A winner isn't nearly as afraid of losing as a loser is secretly afraid of winning.

A winner goes through a problem; a loser goes around it and never gets past it.

Floyd L. Griffin, Jr.

Chapter 7

1st Senate Term (1994 Campaign - end of 1996)

At this time in my life, I had never held a political seat, but I had been thinking about it for some time. I had run for a seat on the Baldwin County Commission and lost the race, though I did very well considering the district was a majority white one. Presently, Wilbur Baugh was the sitting senator in our district. I didn't feel like he was representing our district very well and he had had some run-ins with then Governor Zell Miller, so I traveled throughout the district and talked to several elected officials in different counties to test the climate. After I did this, I felt like I could gain enough support to win the senate seat in the next election.

When I entered the Senate race, not only was I running against incumbent Baugh, but also Marty Fierman, an Eatonton attorney, who incidentally, shared my views about Baugh's ineffectiveness.

The Putnam County Democratic Executive Committee held an open forum at Putnam County High School in Eatonton at which Fierman and I attended, but Baugh was conspicuously absent. It was at this forum that Fierman was asked to clarify a statement he had made recently at the Milledgeville Optimists Club; a statement to the effect that I was not electable because I was black. Said Fierman, "What I said was that in this district, which is 60% white and 40% black, he

(Griffin) would not get enough crossover votes to win. I don't think race is an issue in this election, but in East-Central Georgia it is always a factor," he concluded. Both of his statements were insulting to white voters in our district. He was, in effect, saying that none of the white voters would vote for me because I'm black. There may not have been a race issue, but it almost seemed as if he was creating one.

The first time that all three of us appeared together to speak and answer questions was at a luncheon sponsored by the National Association of Retired Federal Employees. Baugh tried to assert that because neither Fierman nor I had ever held public office, that we were unfit to do so. Fierman also tried to say that my platform was all general issues — no concrete goals, when in fact, I stated at this luncheon that I intended to deal with family values, crime and education.

By May, Senator Baugh was incensed enough about hearing the truth about himself to publicly charge that Fierman and I were "in cahoots" because we both happened to agree that his seat was an empty one. We (Fierman and I) both knew that Baugh was trying to win the race by throwing money at it through advertisements and billboards. He had not once been seen out talking to people; he didn't even seem to have a campaign trail.

My goals and vision if elected were simple and straightforward. I knew that, with the technological age advancing on us, our young people should be properly educated to take their places in the business world. I wanted to promote family values; I knew that restoring our community could only come after restoring our families.

I wanted to stimulate economic development in our area; Milledgeville is rich with Georgia history and tourism; if stimulated, tourism would offer an economic advantage over our present state. There was absolutely no reason why Milledgeville should not be the tourist capitol of Georgia; someone should be capitalizing on the fact that we were the first state capitol of Georgia, not to mention the abundance of antebellum homes and historic sites in our city.

The general election was July 19th and surprisingly, I ended up in a run-off with Senator Baugh, pulling ahead of him by 222 votes. Fierman conceded defeat gracefully and as he had all along, continued to maintain that I would make a much more effective senator than Baugh.

I felt really good about being the first black to be elected to the Georgia Senate from a rural, majority white district. This showed me that the people had voted according to their hearts and minds, not according to race. Evidently, voters realized that good leadership was needed and they just weren't getting it from Wilbur Baugh.

Reflections From Nathalie

Prior to becoming mayor, Floyd served as a state senator. The first week of the session was mostly ceremonial, however activities for spouses were available throughout the session consisting mostly of luncheons, receptions and trips. No one was required to attend or participate and some spouses did not. Even though serving in the state senate was Floyd's first successful venture in the political arena, he was well equipped for the task. He brought to the table a wealth of knowledge, experience, fresh ideas, and most of all a desire to serve and represent the people effectively. His constituents were well served.

In December of 1994, I attended the 19th Biannual Institute for Georgia Legislators held at the University of Georgia in Athens. This was a series of lectures and workshops that introduced me to the legislative process, as well as a wide range of issues facing lawmakers in Georgia, such as economic growth and issues facing the elderly in our state, that I would be dealing with a Senator. There, I met other Senator-elects and Lt Governor Pierre Howard and I was named to the Higher Education and the Health and Human Resources Committees and was chosen to serve on the State and Local Government Operations and the Defense and Veterans Affairs Committees.

I immediately got down to business. Though I wouldn't be officially sworn in until January 9, 1995, the seats that I would hold on four committees were important to Baldwin County. The Health and Human Services Committee would help me be active in meeting the needs of many institutions in Milledgeville, including the Youth Development Campus and the Central State Hospital. Sitting on the Governmental Operations Committee, I planned to work on legislation that would require impact studies when a state agency wants to relocate from one county to another. This was very important to Baldwin County because 36% of people holding jobs in Milledgeville worked for the state. My place on the Defense and Veterans Committee was important because of the Georgia War Veterans Home in Milledgeville, and the Higher Education Committee was also a key seat because our city was the home of Georgia College, Georgia Military College, and soon would be home to Macon Technical Institute.

Once I became Senator, one of my first pieces of legislation that I saw passed was the resolution declaring 1995 to be the "Year of the Family." It was approved 52-0 on the Senate floor, and although it was not enforceable, it emphasized the need to provide for our elderly and to strengthen education of our youth.

In May, (1995) Governor Miller appointed a Commission on Privatization of Government Services as a way to trim his budget. Joe Tanner left his position as head of the Georgia Department of Natural Resources to serve as Executive Director of this commission. Former mayor of Macon George Israel was appointed to chair the nine member bipartisan group. One of the first things this commission did was set out to privatize the Georgia War Veterans Home in Milledgeville.

By summer, (1995) Representative Bobby Parham in the House and I were fighting this bill. In October, a group of veterans and the state Employees Union won a temporary restraining order preventing Governor Zell Miller from privatizing the Georgia War Veterans Home in Milledgeville. This was a four-month temporary order and the state immediately appealed that order to the Georgia

Supreme Court. I felt like the Governor should not have the authority to privatize a large institution like the Veterans Home without seeking permission from the legislature. I wasn't against privatization, per se, but I felt like the legislative branch should be involved.

During a visit in November 1995, to try to convince those involved of the need for privatization of the War Veterans Home, Larry Brockaway, assistant commissioner of the State Department of Veterans Service, was unable to answer even the simplest of questions. Brockaway, and others who supported the bill, maintained that the state would save millions of dollars with privatization, but when asked how the money would be saved, he had to admit that he didn't know. This occasion was a three hour hearing at which four state senators and three representatives listened to testimony from veterans, state officials, employees of the hospital, and other interested parties, at the auditorium of Central State Hospital. To save $8 million in costs by 1998, it was obvious to everyone involved that the privatization would include reducing the staff and therefore, the quality of care that the veterans were currently receiving. This was unacceptable.

The privatization issue carried over into 1996 and in January, the bill that I had introduced to block the privatization of the Veterans Home went to committee on the second day of the 40-day legislative session. I had included in this bill a provision allowing state employees to keep their jobs if the privatization became a reality. Later that week, I introduced legislation addressing privatization on a broader scale.

Also in '96, I introduced a bill to the General Assembly that would regulate the relocation of state offices. In 1993, the Women's Prison had been moved from Milledgeville to Atlanta without enough advance notice and practically no input from the community. Senate Bill 150 would require advance notice of at least 120 days before a state office moved and an impact study would have to be conducted at least 60 days in advance to determine the effect on employees, their families, and the community at-large.

In March, I initiated a bill that would require 96 hours of community service from high school students before they could graduate. This bill brought some very mixed reviews from educators. Linda Shrenko, the new state School Superintendent, applauded the bill's intent, but wanted the community service to be voluntary. She also felt that the bill wouldn't work for everyone; that it might adversely affect smaller systems due to a lack of transportation for the kids or funds to pay someone to coordinate and enforce the requirement. "I believe in local control," Shrenko said. "I just don't believe a one-size-fits-all solution would work."

But the bill was very well received by the Professional Association of Georgia Educators. "It appears to be a bill for students to buy into the community early on and provide opportunities to give something back to the community," said Adrian Baird, PAGE's Director of Professional Services. After talking extensively with Shrenko, I agreed to a Senate resolution in favor of community service as an elective in high school.

In the middle of March, the $10.7 billion 1995-96 state budget passed in the House and the Senate. This was a great victory for me because the budget included $3.5 million to renovate the Old State Capitol building. Governor Miller had wanted to spend $7.8 million on the project, but only part was approved this year. Still, it was a start. Also in the budget was $300,000 to renovate the Old Governor's Mansion at Georgia College and $100,000 in community funds for the chronically mentally ill. I had hoped for $500,000 for the OAMI (Oconee Alliance for the Mentally III), but this was a good beginning. Once you get an initial amount passed, it's much easier the following year to continue with the piece of legislation and improve on it.

Thus, the first legislative season went well. I won a few, lost a few, and compromised on a few.

On June 29th, the United States Supreme Court struck down the majority black 11th Congressional District which runs through Jefferson County. The 11th District, originally drawn in 1992, starts in Atlanta's suburbs and runs about 250 miles across the state to Augusta and Savannah. The Supreme Court ruled that the district lines violated some voters' equal protection rights. In 1994, a three-judge panel declared the 11th District unconstitutional, and now, with the Supreme Court's go-ahead, the lines would be redrawn at the sitting of the General Assembly in August.

The 11th District had been declared unconstitutional because it was a majority black district. The special session for reapportionment began on August 14th and the Senate's first plan for redistricting looked pretty good to me. It would restore Morgan County and remove Warren, Jefferson, and Washington counties. I voted for this plan because it would keep my district compact, with lines clearly drawn. But the plan would have to pass in the House and meet approval by the Justice Department before it became law and though I expected a fair amount of disagreement between the Senate and the House and even among members of each, I was surprised at how unmoving each individual would be in their opinions of how the districts should be drawn. Everyone was in for a long, drawn-out debate.

Eventually, through many days of disagreement about how the lines should be redrawn, the Senate voted to adjourn but the House refused to go along, so we remained in session. Before the Supreme Court struck down the 11th District as being unconstitutional, Georgia had three majority black districts. Louis Farrakhan, the Nation of Islam leader, had been urging us legislators to push to keep all three majority districts. "As long as the districts favored whites, nobody had nothing to say about it....But if a district will give blacks more representation, then they want to take that away," he said. But the longer we argued our points in session, the further away we were from agreement. Then, things went from bad to worse. Democratic Senator Mark Taylor from Albany offered a plan that would break up two of the three majority black districts and provide for one minority influence district. I spoke out against this plan because I felt that it was worse than the map the Supreme Court had ruled unconstitutional.

In September, the Georgia legislature abandoned efforts to come up with a solution for redrawing the districts; most legislators, myself included, felt it was better to give up than to allow divisions to become so bad that they caused permanent damage to already strained relationships. After five weeks with no solution in sight and over $500,000 in expenses, we finally threw the task to the courts. Mark Taylor's plan was adopted and Morgan County moved out of the 24th District and into the 25th (my district), effective after the 1996 elections.

In November, I chaired a study committee in response to a large amount of bad press about a crisis in the Hancock County School System. We heard testimony that state auditors found that "purely improper expenditures" had been occurring for an extended amount of time. The audit showed that the school system had a deficit of $1.68 million in its general fund — up from $1.39 million the previous year. They also had a $162,000 deficit in their food services account. The auditors found that three employees had been paid a total of $8,672 for unused annual leave and that two other employees had been given salary advances of $4,407, both practices of which are violations of the state constitution. Also discovered was the fact that Nicholas Antone had continued to receive an annual salary of $57,601 after the school board had voted the year before to cut costs by abolishing his position as director of administrative and operational services. The push to fire long-time Superintendent Marvin Lewis had resulted in his resignation in August, despite the fact that the board had already voted to fire him on grounds of financial mismanagement.

In January of 1996, I introduced legislation that would keep intact Georgia Military College's local Board of Trustees and drop the late Senator Culver Kidd's plan for creating a larger board from statewide individuals. In the early 1990s, Kidd had twice tried to change the makeup of the board to include members from around the state. In 1991, the U.S. Justice Department had rejected Culver's bill after which he came back the next year with a bill that would include board members from each of the state's congressional districts. The second bill was never rejected by the Justice Department, but it was not approved either. My bill would limit membership on the board of trustees to the mayor of Milledgeville and one member from each of the six voting districts in the city. This new legislature also eliminated some of the requirements that scholarships awarded at GMC be based on financial need and student achievement. It would give the board of trustees sole responsibility for establishing the guidelines by which scholarships would be rewarded. I felt very good about the fact that this bill passed unanimously in the Senate.

During this General Assembly, Lt. Pierre Howard chose me to serve on the Blue Ribbon Commission, a special legislative panel that would examine the General Assembly operations and make recommendations for its improvement to the General Assembly in 1998. I was honored to be chosen and saw this appointment as an excellent opportunity to look at some of the age-old traditions of legislators and whether or not these traditions were still in our best interests. For example, the General Assembly session is a 40-day annual session that runs from January to March each year. This dates back to when Georgia was primarily an agricultural state and the length and season of the session was a convenience to legislator/farmers. I was, and still am, of the opinion that the Assembly needs more than 40 days to take care of its business.

Also in January, Governor Miller's proposal to privatize the Georgia War Veterans Home, again came up for discussion in the Senate State and Local Government Operations Committee. This time, when the bill was placed on the Senate floor for a vote, it was shot down by the rest of the Senate in a vote of 14-39 against my bill; just a few hours after the Senate had given Governor Miller the go-ahead to privatize three new state prisons. In an attempt to block this, a motion was filed in the Baldwin County Superior Court stating that unless Judge William Prior extends his October 19, 1995 order for another 120 days, Governor Miller would go ahead with privatization before the courts or Legislature have had their final say on the issue. I requested the opinion of Attorney General Michael Bowers on the legality of the Executive branch's decision to privatize the Home without approval of the General Assembly.

Because my bill had been shot down on the Senate floor, I then introduced a bill that I called a "contingency plan" that would guarantee legislative oversight in the event that the plan for privatization was successful. This contingency plan would guarantee a high quality of care for the veterans housed at the facility and ensure that the proposed savings were being met.

By May of 1996, five companies had showed interest in bidding on the contract to privately manage the Georgia War Veterans Home, but with the entire furor over privatization, all but one company, UHSPruitt, had backed off, unwilling to take on the trouble that might be coming. Priva Trends, a subsidiary of Pruitt Corp. of Toccoa, was awarded the $13.7 million contract. Though there was some concern because the Pruitt Corporation had contributed $2,500 to Governor Miller's campaign, this wasn't given much credence because the contribution was made well in advance of any talk about privatizing the War Veterans Home. Additionally, Pruitt had been in business for more than 25 years, managing 29 nursing homes and retirement centers around the state.

This General Assembly also saw my introduction of legislature that would require training for financial officers in the state's public school system in light of the fiasco in Hancock County in 1995. This 4-part bill, if passed, would require school systems to employ at least one full time accountant or send their bookkeeping/accounting staff to a six-course program offered by the University of Georgia's Carl Vinson Institute. Also included in the bill was a requirement that the chief financial officers of any school in debt submit a plan to the state for getting out of debt, and give the local school board a monthly report itemizing all expenses, which each member of the school board must sign. The Senate passed 3 of the 4 bills, with the exception of the bill requiring minimum training in accounting for any school system employee who handles the financial records.

In June, qualifying began for the next Senate term. Although many incumbents drew no opposition this time, I faced two challengers for my seat. Ben Stewart, owner of a finance and insurance company in Union Point and mayor of that city for the previous 17 years, was my opponent in the Democratic primary. Whoever won this primary would face Republican newcomer Bob Lackey of Monticello. Lackey was vice president of marketing for Southeastern Die Company in Lithonia.

Right off the bat, I questioned Stewart's loyalties. I was aware that in March, just two months before qualifying as a Democrat against me in the Senate race, he had contributed $500 to the campaign of Republican Congressman Charlie Norwood of Augusta. He also tried to start a mud-slinging contest by making an issue of my disagreement with Governor Miller on privatizing the War Veterans Home. Stewart is, himself, against privatization. I merely thought that more study was needed before the move to ensure continued quality patient care and the protection of staff members' positions. Stewart's claim was that I had alienated Governor Miller by disagreeing with him. To my way of thinking, this just meant that, if elected Senator, Stewart would not stand up for his beliefs if it meant angering or alienating someone of high standing. This was a candidate we did not need in the Senate.

I had accomplished many of my objectives during my first term as Senator. I had introduced and passed 8 bills, including three that dealt with the financial operations of the public school system, legislation that was badly needed after the Hancock County School's fiasco. Also introduced by me and passed was a bill designating 1995 as The Year of the Family and another that determined the composition of the Georgia Military College Board of Trustees.

Also while Senator, I had appropriated over $10 million for my district for the years 1996-1997, including $3.5 million for the renovation of the Old Capitol Building in Milledgeville. These accomplishments were nothing to sneeze at and I was proud of the things I had gotten done in less than two years.

In any event, I won the primary, beating Stewart by a margin of nearly 3-2 in all but two counties. Bob Lackey, my Republican opponent, ran his entire campaign by writing letters to newspapers throughout the district, criticizing my political record. He had nothing to say about his own qualifications or background and thought to beat me by running a smear campaign. Thankfully, the voters saw through this and re-elected the right man for the job.

July 1, 1996 saw the privatization of the Georgia War Veterans Home. Priva Trends named three top managers to run the home; Raymond Masneri to be Executive Director and to manage the Wheeler Building; Melvin Moses to run the Wood Building; and Laird G. Leeder to manage the Russell Building. All three men were licensed nursing home administrators and had already been working with Priva Trends.

Senator Culver Kidd, an institution in the Senate, had passed away last December after a battle with chronic anemia at the age of 81. Because Senator Kidd was from Milledgeville and I had a great amount of respect for this man who had served in the General Assembly for 42 years, I put forth a resolution to place a portrait of him in the Senate area on the third floor of the Capitol. The vote to pass this resolution was only a formality, as 50 of the 56 members of the Senate had signed on as co-sponsors of the bill. The resolution stated that "The exceptional parliamentary skill and savvy political style of this former member will long be remembered and respected by his colleagues. His accomplishments and contributions deserve recognition and honor." These remarks were actually an understatement, as Senator Culver Kidd was one of the greatest Senators who had ever lived.

About this time, Representative Bobby Parham and I heard of plans to move the forensic services from Central State Hospital in Milledgeville to Macon. The forensic unit is where the state mental health system evaluates and treats criminals before their trials. It also treats prisoners with mental problems. Housed in the Binion Building, the forensic unit had fended off prior attempts to have it moved; in 1982 and in 1994, after which a task force was appointed to study the needs. This task force, our best weapon in keeping the unit in Milledgeville, was appointed by the Commissioner and the Board of the Department of Human Resources.

Obviously, we were very pleased when Governor Miller's proposed budget for 1997 included $605,000 to plan a new forensics unit at Central State Hospital. If the legislature were to agree to that, then Miller would propose another $15 million the following year to build the new facility. This was 75% of the battle. The other 25% would be working between the House and the Senate; Representative Parham would keep it in the House budget and I would keep it in the Senate budget.

Around the end of 1996, Georgia State Corrections Commissioner Wayne Garner handed out pink slips to 235 prison teachers for Christmas, alerting them that their jobs would vanish on January 31, 1997. This caught my attention, as well as that of House Appropriations Committee Chairman Terry Coleman from Eastman. We asked for hearings on the firings and became aware that Coleman, Governor Zell Miller, House Speaker Tom Murphy, and Lt Governor Pierre Howard had been discussing the firings for about a week prior.

The hearing would serve as a request that Garner keep the teachers on the payroll until August of 1997. This would give them time to seek other jobs in a market that is very competitive in this state. I wanted more from this hearing, however; I wanted Garner to justify the firings. I felt that we needed to consider the impact the firings would have, not just on the employees, but on the inmates, as well. In the past, inmates were able to get their high school diplomas (GEDs) in the program and I wondered if this would continue to be the case. Twenty-seven of the 235 teachers were employed in Baldwin County prisons, so this issue was close to home for me.

Garner's justification for the firings was that with new $20 an hour contract teachers, the state would not have to provide state health insurance or retirement, an expected $8 million savings to the state annually. Though this was commendable, it still didn't justify the way the firings were handled. I felt like we needed to look into this issue much deeper.

Having beat Ben Stewart in the primary and Bob Lackey in November, I was ready to start a new year on the Senate floor. I still had some items on the table that weren't resolved and I wanted to see them through to the end. Thus ended my first term as Senator for the 25th District of the State of Georgia.

ALICE MITCHELL INTERVIEW

Alice Mitchell and Floyd Griffin attended school together from the fifth grade through the twelfth and have been friends and neighbors throughout those years. "Floyd has always been competitive and bright," said Mitchell. "He always got along with people. Never got into fights."

Griffin left for college about the time that Mitchell and her husband Leon went to New York. "I didn't see Floyd for some 20-odd years, and when he came back, I was really impressed by what he had become," she said.

Mitchell also worked for Griffin's campaign during his Senate runs. "Nathalie and I (Griffin's wife) worked together as volunteers," she said. "When he would come back into town, he would just jump right in and do whatever needed to be done. He was always very appreciative of the things that people did for him—always thanking them. I admire Floyd Griffin; he is all about helping people—all people."

Leon Mitchell Interview

Leon Mitchell, husband of Alice Mitchell, was a year ahead of Floyd Griffin in school. "I know Floyd best from his Senate runs. I was his campaign manager, so I traveled with him," said Mitchell. "He was so loaded with energy and enthusiasm that it would rub off on me. Sometimes, Floyd would question who was actually running for the seat," laughed Mitchell. "Initially, I had no desire to get into politics, but he so stirred my interest that I ended up feeling great about it."

"Floyd is a very caring person and very no-nonsense," continued Mitchell. "I saw that Floyd was determined to make a difference and his community got what they needed when Floyd was in his seat.

"I'll tell you, Floyd's running in a majority white district and winning really changed my opinion about an African American running for office in the South."

Senator Robert Brown with Senator and Mrs. Griffin

Chapter 8

2nd Senate Term (1996 - 1998)

1997 began much as 1996 ended; back to the job at hand. First item on the table as we went into the General Assembly session was the resolution that legislators take Wednesdays off as a day of rest. This resolution had passed the House with no fanfare by a large margin, and then passed in the Senate after a lengthy discussion.

Governor Miller presented the House and Senate with his proposed $11.8 billion budget, committing over 55% to education throughout the state. In this budget, my district would receive $4.8 million to renovate Herty Hall at Georgia College & State University; $4.5 million to finish renovation on the Old Capitol building at Georgia Military College; over $300,000 to repair and renovate buildings at the War Veterans Home; nearly $4 million to renovate the Bill Ireland Youth Development Center in Milledgeville; and $359,000 for planning and design funds for the Old Governors Mansion on the grounds of the Georgia College & State University. I was grateful for Governor Miller's support for the various projects I had going in my area. This would be nearly $15 million appropriated for my district, a tremendous improvement over the previous year. This budget also seemed to put an end to the debate over whether the new prison psychiatric hospital would stay in Milledgeville or move to Macon. The Governor's budget would nearly double the bed space at the hospital.

After adjustments, the budget also included some much needed funds for local projects. There would now be $10,000 for Milledgeville's Main Street Downtown Development; $15,000 for the Baldwin County Council on Substance Abuse; $18,000 for the Rape Crisis Center; and $10,000 for the Milledgeville-Baldwin County museum project. This was a tremendous success and reflects how well Representative Bobby Parham and I worked together. Milledgeville is Rep Parham's hometown as well, and with his being in the House and me in the Senate, we were able to push through several items that were in our area's interest. If he couldn't get it through the House, I tried to push it through the Senate. This team effort was very successful in getting funds appropriated for Milledgeville, as well as the rest of our district.

Despite the fact that Governor Miller was successful in seeing the Georgia War Veterans Home privatized, I did get some consolation when my bill requiring that state agencies give legislators 60 days notice before contracting to privatize, passed in the Senate by a vote of 43-7. The House then unanimously passed the bill. With a few minor adjustments in the wording of the bill between the House and Senate versions, it would then go to Governor Miller to sign into law. This was a great victory for me. The privatization issue had been a struggle between the Governor and me and this was a resolution that satisfied both of us. I have to give Governor Miller credit for working with me and Representative Parham on this to a conclusion that was agreeable to everyone. In effect, the bill required that the speaker of the House and the lieutenant governor be notified 60 days in advance before any state agency is turned over to private business.

Also on the floor of the Senate was a bill that would eliminate the requirement that candidates for school superintendent have three years teaching experience. Republicans considered this a slap at state school superintendent Linda Shrenko, who was the state's first Republican superintendent. Written by Senator Mary Oliver, this bill would ostensibly help her constituent, Joe Martin, who would likely be a candidate in the next election for superintendent. This was irrelevant in my opinion; the point was that the law restricted the position to teachers only. In effect, it says that, even with all my years as a colonel and businessman, I'm not qualified to run. That's ludicrous; the state superintendent should be like a CEO.

In February, the issue of state-owned land in Baldwin came up. At that time, the state of Georgia owned more than 8,000 acres of land here and was expressing an interest in selling it, so I introduced a resolution establishing a committee of legislators and private citizens to recommend a plan to sell off the land. I did this because Joe Tanner, director of the privatization committee, had asked the Milledgeville-Baldwin County Chamber of Commerce to make recommendations on how to proceed with this land sale. The only notice provided to me and Representative Bobby Parham was a copy of the committee's letter to Tanner. By then, we were in the middle of a session and I felt like I was just being told, "this is what we want and you need to do it." Well, I don't work like that; I don't just draw up resolutions and bills because someone tells me to. I have to know what's going on because I have to answer to my constituents for my actions. I don't just jump on anyone's bandwagon. I felt like legislators should be kept abreast of the entire process, since it would be us that would be introducing and supporting any bills concerning land sales.

Personally, I favored the sale of state-owned land and that's why I introduced my own resolution concerning this. I wanted the process to be carried out openly and fairly, with the citizens opinions aired in the process. Since this was not done yet, I didn't support legislation to carry out the proposal of the Milledgeville-Baldwin County Chamber of Commerce. Instead, I chaired a panel that included legislators, a top aide to Governor Miller, the Chamber of Commerce chairman, and others. I felt much better about the situation then because it seemed that all involved felt like we were going about it the right way, especially incoming Milledgeville-Baldwin County Chamber of Commerce chairperson Randy Weaver. Thus, when we made a recommendation the following year, we could feel confident that the legislators would defend our resolution. We held our first meeting in July.

In March, I acquired the approval of an FY Supplemental Budget of $66,000 for Taliaferro County, a small county in my district that was in need of improvement in their safety responses for their citizens. This money included $54,000 for a new fire truck and $12,000 for a new Sheriff's sedan. These improvements for Taliaferro County led directly to better response times and better safety conditions for the county. Thus went the year 1997 on the floor of the General Assembly.

By 1998, I had new issues on the table as well as some unfinished business to take care of. In January, I started a statewide campaign to raise the state's minimum wage of $3.25 to meet the federal minimum wage of $5.15. The current minimum wage of $3.25 only applied to businesses that grossed between $40,000 and $499,000 annually and although they were few in number, this lower wage affected about 135,000 people. Because of welfare reform, this was not a livable wage. I was pushing legislation that would raise the minimum wage incrementally over the next three to five years, until it reached the federal level. Unfortunately, this resolution was shot down on the Senate floor by a vote of 35-19 in February.

On or about January 10th, Lt. Governor Howard appointed me chair of the Senate's Committee on Interstate Cooperation. Although this committee was not one of the higher profile committees, I was, nevertheless, honored that Howard felt I was qualified for the job. This was particularly significant for me because this was my last year as a Senator and I would be running for the seat of Lt. Governor in the next election.

In February, I wrote Senate Bill 420 in an effort to help Georgia's dairy farmers. Because of rising production costs, farmers had to import more costly milk from other states. Bill 420 would enable Georgia's dairy farmers to join the Southern Dairy Compact Commission, a 15-state group that had the authority to set a minimum price they would accept for their milk. At that time, farmers were receiving about $1.16 per gallon, down from $1.26 in 1983. Dairy farmers were going under at a rapid rate and this was one of the reasons. My bill set a cap of $1.50 per gallon and Bill 420 passed in the Senate by a vote of 36-17. It then went to the House of Representatives. There the bill sat for about three weeks in the House Rules Committee where Chairman Bill Lee from Forest Park had some reservations. Eventually, though, the bill passed in the House by a vote of 130-44.

I also proposed a constitutional amendment that would eliminate state and local taxes on livestock for farmers. This amendment passed 50-2 in the Senate and went to the House for consideration.

At some point during this General Assembly, I introduced a resolution to name the huge kitchen at Central State Hospital after House Representative Bobby Parham. He was one of the facility's chief supporters and had been instrumental in securing $8 million to fund this kitchen, which prepares 25,000 meals a day to feed mental health patients and prisoners all over the state. This resolution passed unanimously by a vote of 45-0 and if passed in the House, would secure a plaque bearing Parham's name to be displayed in the kitchen. This was something that I wanted to do for Bobby. He had represented Baldwin County and Milledgeville for some 20 years and nothing had ever been named after him. This was my way of showing appreciation for all that he had done over the years.

The Senate also passed my legislation to sell 72 state-owned houses near Central State Hospital as well as several pieces of property near the Bill Ireland Youth Development Center. This was a package of three resolutions and received unanimous support from the Senate. This land was part of the same 8,000 acres of state-owned land that the Milledgeville-Baldwin County Chamber of Commerce had tried to sell the year before without involving legislators, after which I formed a study committee to handle the sales. The resolutions would now go to the House of Representatives.

In April, Governor Miller vetoed my bill that would have allowed Georgia to join other southern states in the Southern Dairy Compact. In his statement, he said that the bill constituted price fixing and would have caused milk prices to go up. Many couldn't understand this move on his part. My bill had set a price cap of $1.50 a gallon, a slight raise in price that the dairy farmers of Georgia badly needed to stay afloat. Senator Harold Ragan of Cairo was particularly upset. "Prices are determined by supply and demand, and if we lose our dairy farmers, we'll have higher prices," Ragan said. "We're already consuming two million more gallons than we are producing.

We have a deficit now." This was a terrible blow to the dairy industry in Georgia. It is important to note here that in 1999, after becoming Governor, Roy Barnes signed the legislation that allowed Georgia to join the Southern Dairy Compact. But approval from Congress would still be needed.

"I met Floyd Griffin when he came to the Senate in the 1990s," said Senator Robert Brown. "He would study an issue and once he made up his mind, he made his position known, and then prevailed. Floyd is a very independent spirit; honest and straightforward to a fault. He has always been willing to do whatever is necessary to stand up for what he believes in and he speaks his mind despite the consequences."

Run For Lieutenant Governor
(1997 – 1998)

I decided during May 1997 that I would run for Lieutenant Governor and succeed Pierre Howard, who would be running for the Governor's seat in 1998. I was hoping to make history as the first African American Lt. Governor in the state of Georgia. I made the announcement on my birthday, May 24th at 1:00 A.M. on the Capitol steps in Atlanta and at 3pm on the steps of the Old Capitol Building at Georgia Military College.

The list of candidates was long this time, with 11 running for the seat; six Democrats and five Republicans. I was joined by Nick Dodys, Guy Middleton, Mary Margaret Oliver, Mark Taylor and last minute candidate, Public Service Commissioner Mac Barber on the Democratic ticket. The Republican ticket had five candidates: Senators Chuck Clay and Pam Glanton; Rockdale County Commission Chairman Randy Poynter; Clint Day; and Fulton County Commission Chairman Mitch Skandalakis. Of everyone in the running, I was the only African American.

In June, I began a nine-city tour of campaigning that began in Augusta and ended with a press conference at City Hall in Macon. It was there that I announced that my primary focus for this campaign would be improvement in education. I spoke about my 12-point plan that would call for more after school programs and the use of retired military personnel to improve school discipline.

In July of 1998, U.S. Representative John Lewis, a Democrat from Atlanta, endorsed me for Lt. Governor. "Georgia needs the leadership, the vision, and the experience of Floyd Griffin," he said. "I know Floyd Griffin can win this campaign and make history." Others that endorsed me in this race included United Nations ambassador and former Atlanta mayor Andrew Young as my honorary campaign chairman, U.S. Representative Cynthia McKinney, state Representative and President of GABEO (Georgia Association of Black Elected

Officials) Tyrone Brooks, and Fulton County Commissioner Michael Hightower.

My focus during the campaign was better education. It was my feeling that retired military personnel (generally around 40 years of age) could make a significant contribution to education in this state as teachers, if we could offer them the right benefit package.

My biggest problem during the campaign was the lack of funds. While my opponents racked up nearly a million dollars apiece, I was trying to run a campaign on barely $150,000. This made for a lot of traveling around the state in my own car rather than flying; I couldn't do any mass mailings or yard signs and I couldn't afford to pay any campaign workers. Also detrimental was the lack of a TV ad campaign. However, I did show up for any debate or forum that I could possibly get to, including an NAACP forum in Atlanta, and a black press forum in Macon.

In October, GABEO met in Milledgeville at my church, Trinity CME, despite the fact that I didn't make the run-off for Lt. Governor. Tyrone Brooks was present, as well as many of Georgia's black elected officials and civil rights leaders from around the state. The purpose of the convention was to explore voter apathy among blacks over the course of the weekend of October 30tn and 31st.

After losing the race for Lt. Governor in 1998, I seriously considered running for the Senate seat again. I had realized success in many endeavors during my terms as Senator, and at the same time, I felt as though I had unfinished business as a legislator. I guess I really wanted to serve Middle Georgia again. After much thought and a lot of talking to Nathalie and many others, I decided to run again, and I lost.

Beyond The Senate

During my quest to become the first black lieutenant governor of Georgia, I raised and spent more than $160 thousand dollars in my bid for election, while my opponent in the race spent several millions. Still, when all was said and done, there was only a difference of 38,000 votes between me and the top vote getter. If I had raised more money to get TV ads, it would have shown people throughout the state that an African American was running for election. Still, I came in at number one in 22 counties and second in the Atlanta metropolitan area.

We thought the time for change was right, but all of Georgia was not yet ready to elect a person of color as Lt. Governor. My campaign was under-capitalized. To get the media exposure we needed, it was going to cost considerably more money than we had. Secondly, we just couldn't get blacks to come out in large enough numbers to vote. This apathy was not because blacks didn't know I was a candidate of color—because many did. I believe that many were apathetic because of the Willie Lynch Syndrome, the name African Americans give to a mentality that afflicts some blacks; a crabs-in-the-barrel behavior that divides descendents of American slavery on the basis of frivolous differences and makes them resistant toward those blacks who try to succeed, or crawl up out of life's "barrel" in a quest for improvement.

Mayor Griffin introducing Beverly Calhoun. Rear: Annie Miller and Mrs. Nathalie Griffin

Chapter 9

Hometown Mayor

I really never had any intention to run for local office again. I decided to run because I was encouraged by some concerned local citizens, basically black women. I agonized for at least a month over this, during which time open meetings were being held with concerned black citizens. I attended these meetings to be sure I had the black support.

Beverly W. Calhoun was one of the ladies of the original core group that was pushing me to run for mayor. Mrs. Calhoun is a local community activist in the city of Milledgeville. "We had changed from an at-large voting format into a district voter system and my group and I felt that we had a good chance of electing a black mayor at this time," said Mrs. Calhoun in an interview. "I already knew Floyd because we both grew up on the south side of town," she said. "We contacted other established black groups in town and began holding open meetings to discuss the possibility of electing Floyd. He was well-respected and we had all known him throughout his military and political career as well as his business at Slater's Funeral Home." Several of these open meetings were held at DeVonte's, owned by Mrs. Doris Watson. "Devonte's was a building that Mrs. Watson rented out to groups who needed a place to meet. It was a really nice place; she had smaller rooms for birthday parties and larger rooms for conventions and such," Calhoun added.

An average of 50 people attended these meetings, which were open forum in nature, I guess you could say. I can remember only one person that showed some concern about my running for mayor and that was city councilman Richard "Boo" Mullins. I've never figured out why he disliked me so, but that man was a burr in my side during the entire time I was mayor. If I said "left," he said "right." If I said it was sunny outside, he would insist that it was raining. Despite Mullins' contempt, it was obvious that I had plenty of support in the black community. I finally decided to give it a shot.

I announced my intention to run for mayor of Milledgeville at the beginning of September. I had made the decision to do this and I felt I was in it all the way. I had plenty of support, but my biggest supporter was Nathalie. She believed in me as she always has, so felt like I couldn't lose. The Milledgeville Union-Recorder ran the story on Tuesday, September 4, 2001 and we held a campaign kick-off at Walter B. Williams, Jr. Park the day before. I remember it rained that day, but it didn't matter at all to me; I was on cloud nine. We had a big cookout; barbequed a hog and had hamburgers and hotdogs with all the fixings. When it was raining, we just got under the picnic shelters. We gave away t-shirts to the first 200 registered voters and we ran out long before it was over. We had nearly 400 people that day.

I shook a lot of hands and talked to a lot people about what I felt were Milledgeville's biggest issues. I felt the city government needed to be reorganized and that with teamwork, this vision was a very real possibility.

I didn't want to run as a black candidate; I felt that it really was a non-issue. Blacks and whites alike had encouraged me to run and race just didn't enter into the picture for me. I saw a need that I felt like I could fill and I knew that my years in the military and politics had given me the experience I needed to be a good mayor. In fact, I think one of the reasons I had so much support was that I was genuinely interested in how the general public felt about key issues and wanted to hear their opinions and feelings on a very basic level.

The tragic events of the World Trade Center, Pennsylvania and the Pentagon terroristic plane attacks of September 11, 2001 had a very real impact on me. I guess the best way to describe it would be to say that I was completely shocked. I don't think anyone thinks about something like that happening, so when it did, I think the nation was just paralyzed for awhile. It was one of those events where everyone can remember where they were and what they were doing when it happened. I was at my business making funeral arrangements. We didn't have a TV there, but when I walked into my secretary's office that morning, she told me. At that time, only two of the planes had hit. We decided to close the business early and go home to watch it on TV. As soon as I had a free moment, I called my friend, Margaret Hitchcock in New York, to see if she was okay. "I live in Manhattan and I had taken the day off to go shopping and to vote," Margaret recalled of the tragedy. "The plane crashes started while I was still out, but I didn't know it at the time," she said. "When I got home, I turned on the TV and saw it about the time Floyd called me. I was so glad he called because I was just devastated; I had friends that worked there." Hitchcock is still haunted by other sensory memories of that day. "I live near the hospital in an exclusive high rise about 100 short city blocks from the Twin Towers. I heard ambulances all day and night and about 1:00 am the next morning, I had my window cracked and suddenly, smelled raw meat burning. I'm thinking that someone is burning their food until I realized that the stench was coming from the towers. It was just awful," she remembered.

We had just had the press conference on the steps of City Hall the morning before the 911 terrorist attacks. It was the first day to qualify for the mayoral run, among other seats up for election. I had two opponents in this race, incumbent Mayor Johnny Grant, Jr. and Richard Bentley, owner of Wilkinson Insurance.

Mayor Grant wasn't particularly worrisome to me as an opponent. He owned J.C. Grant Company, a local jewelry store, and had spent 23 years on the city council before becoming mayor of Milledgeville. Normally, this would be considered a decent adversary, but not in this case. When he was elected mayor, he had no electable opponents. His administration was predictable and his son-in-law (city councilman Ken Vance) was the shadow mayor; Ken did Grant's bidding. I really didn't think he was all that hot and I knew I could beat him.

On the other hand, Richard Bentley was making his first appearance on Milledgeville's political scene. He was a political neophyte that the good ole' boys recruited because they didn't want a black mayor, and they were tired of Grant's ineptness.

THE CAMPAIGN TRAIL

During my deliberations about whether or not to run, one thing I had to consider was a run-off and I felt that it would be between Bentley and me. Obviously, my greatest concern was trying to win the primary. I had been in one run-off in the Senate race and I didn't want to do it again.

"Boo" Mullins wasn't the only unsupportive person during my campaign; Cedric Davis was another. Davis was a black attorney in Milledgeville; his father was the late Oscar Davis, Sr., the first black to be elected to the Baldwin County Board of Commissioners and a strong past supporter of my political career. He was also one of the first supporters to make a contribution to my first Senate run and he endorsed my candidacy in that race. Oscar's son, Cedric, was a member of one of my two fraternities and Masonic brother. In fact, when he applied to my fraternity, he asked me for a letter of recommendation, which I gladly submitted because of his father. When I announced my run for mayor, Cedric supported Bentley and I was very disappointed. I felt like he should have at least stayed quiet if he wasn't going to support me, because of our fraternity connection. Of course, Cedric and "Boo" Mullins are first cousins.

We worked hard during the campaign and I shook a lot of hands. I had some very concrete plans for the city and I just wanted to get out there and let the public know what those plans were. We had "Griffin's Pledge" postcards made up and we must have distributed thousands of them. All of the cards described my platform and some had my background, while others had my plans for the first 60 days in office if I were elected. We had just less than two months to win this election and I was determined to reach as many potential voters as possible.

I believe that my determination to be easily accessible to the citizens of Milledgeville with my intentions for the city sort of pushed the other candidates to do likewise. At the very least, I had them on their toes. We held an Election Forum on October 25, 2001 at the Baldwin High School auditorium so that we could answer questions that the citizens had about our intentions.

Another event that I think helped the public see what each of us had to offer the city of Milledgeville was Open Market Day on Saturday, October 20, 2001. Open Market Day was a monthly open-air market that drew a great number of people, perhaps the majority of the city on some Saturdays. I felt like this was an opportunity unequaled by any other for public relations.

We also held a "Get Out the Vote" rally on November 4th at Oak Hill Middle School. I really wanted to get as many supporters to the polls as possible. Sometimes, this meant getting people registered who had never voted before. It's one thing to support a candidate; you can do that with all your heart. But if you don't vote or are not even registered to vote, then you do your candidate absolutely no good at all. There was a senior citizen dynamic in Milledgeville that supported me wholeheartedly, most knowing me from childhood. But many of these supporters were not registered to vote. I know that Beverly Calhoun will never forget Miss Matilda Brooks. "Miss Brooks was 99 years old when she registered to vote for the first time in her life, just so that she could vote for Floyd," said Calhoun. "She had known him all his life and was a staunch supporter. She campaigned relentlessly, successfully encouraging many other seniors to get registered. She was so cute, a feisty little thing. She's passed away since then, but was so glad that she got to see Floyd elected," continued Calhoun. "I believe she was more excited than Floyd when he won the seat."

Reflections From Nathalie

When he decided to seek the office of mayor, I thought this would be an excellent opportunity for him to continue and even expand on that desire to serve in his own home town. It was an opportunity to make a difference. Floyd has always looked at a new or different situation as an opportunity, not a problem. He had a clear vision of the direction he thought the city should move and ideas about how to achieve that goal.

I sigh when I think of being First Lady of a city; it was a little frustrating for me. Prior to being a mayor, Floyd was a state senator and there was not a whole lot that the spouses had to do, as far as being involved in activities goes, except during the first week in office, which consisted of a lot of luncheons, trips and ceremonies. But there was nothing that I was really required to do as a senator's wife. However, it was different in the mayor's office. Even though there were no real requirements for the wives, I still found myself cast into the spotlight, whether I wanted to be or not, because my husband was the first black mayor of Milledgeville.

Election Day

Election Day was November 6, 2001. I won the general election by only 78 votes and although I was excited, I was also disappointed at how close the election was. Now, there would be a run-off between me and Richard Bentley. I was shocked that so many whites would vote for someone without qualifications just because he was white. It is also my opinion that anytime a qualified African American is running in a majority white area where a black has never held the seat, the blacks should all support and vote for the African American. We could have won the general election if more blacks had voted for me instead the other two candidates. There were plenty of blacks (including elected officials) that supported and voted for Grant and Bentley.

During those three weeks, we really pounded the pavement. Only 37% of Milledgeville's registered voters had turned out for the election and I (and Bentley, as well) wanted to see a bigger turn-out for the run-off, although this is not usually the case. This run-off, however, bucked the trend, with 44% of the city's 6,906 registered voters turning out. Major special emphasis had been placed on getting the blacks back to the polls and the absentee ballots to the run-off. If it had not been for Julia Ingram and Beverly Calhoun, who went out and got the absentee ballots, I would not have become mayor. This was their expertise. We won by 21 votes because of absentee ballots (I received 214 to Bentley's 88) and due to the closeness of the race, I knew we were going to have some major challenges in governing. This later proved to be true.

We had a great celebration at Devonte's that night. As I spoke to the press, I wanted to stress how the election was a defining moment in Milledgeville's history. My campaign promise of moving the city to the next level had already been realized with my election to the seat of Mayor. In 198 years - Milledgeville's entire history - we had never had a black mayor. This was especially significant to me because Milledgeville was the old capitol city and I felt that we needed to set an example for the whole state. We didn't, albeit by a very close margin. I also stated to the press that our theme for the next year would be "A Bold, New Attitude." I felt this reflected the need for a positive outlook and a brighter, more efficient future for Milledgeville.

One of the first things I announced was that the swearing-in for me and the incoming council members would be held publicly, in a place large enough for everyone who wanted to come. There were too many people involved in this campaign and it just didn't seem right to hold it behind closed doors. This would also show the public that I was serious about holding open forum meetings often, so that I would be aware of the citizen's feelings and opinions on how the city was being run. We held the swearing-in at Central State Hospital Auditorium at 4pm on New Year's Eve and about 600 people attended. Georgia Supreme Court Justice Hugh Thompson, who had grown up in Milledgeville, performed the swearing-in. By this time, I had met with all city department heads and city council members and during the inauguration, I called on them to work with me to achieve this vision I had for a bold new attitude for Milledgeville. I also let everyone know that I felt like doing business as usual would be a prescription for failure. I announced a press conference for January 2, to talk publicly about reorganizing the city government and to announce the department heads for the city.

There had been some talk that I would have 100% blacks running the city of Milledgeville and I suspect that most of this came from the whites who opposed my becoming mayor. This was absolutely not true. I just wanted to go out and find the best qualified individuals to help me realize my goals. I didn't care if they were black, white, Hispanic, whatever. I wanted everyone in the city to have a say in how it would be run. The best way to do this would be to have a diverse, color-blind administration. In fact, 7 of the 11 interim appointments that we announced at the press conference were individuals that were already in those positions. However, anyone that I would have control over that didn't want to work to move Milledgeville forward would have to move on. It wasn't long before that statement became a reality; City Marshall Charles Osborne would be moving on. I had decided that the office of City Marshall needed to be divided in two. It was just too big and I couldn't see paying anyone in that position $62,000 to ineffectively run an office. I offered to appoint Osborne for the first six months of 2002 while I restructured that position, but he declined. He would be the first to go.

In fact, the first two months in office were very hectic. I was filling three roles every day — that of mayor, city administrator, and continuing to run my family business at the funeral home. I had pledged a list of nine things I would do in the first 60 days if elected and I was determined to do them. Within the first month, I had cleared six of the nine objectives from my list. I hired Danny Brown on January 2nd as personnel director, appointed Jo Ann Lunsford as my community affairs officer and special assistant, re-organized the structure of the city government, held our first open dialogue night, became part of an interim youth development council, and met with several key state leaders. Unfortunately, appointing a city administrator was the only one on the list that was out of reach right then. We just didn't have the money and I was reluctant to put the city in a financial bind. When I came into office, the city of Milledgeville was $1.5 million in debt. Within the first year, we were in the black.

Soon after arriving in office, I was very surprised (and proud) to receive an award presented to me by the James Wimberly Institute of Black Studies and History, based in Macon, Georgia. This organization was founded in 1998 and its president was the Reverend Henry Ficklin, a Macon city councilman at the time. I was one of 26 people awarded their 2002 Racial Barrier Breakers Award during their Black History Month celebration. The plaque is beautiful and I still have it. It has a judge's gavel at the top and underneath, it reads: "For the extraordinary achievement of being the first African American mayor of Milledgeville and having the courage to break the previous all white racial barrier, becoming a symbol of hope and a beacon for the future." I was both humbled and empowered by this; I felt I had a purpose to fill and I was determined, more than ever, to fill it.

One of the highlights of my early months in office came as a reception at the Historic Hogg house in Milledgeville. The home has been standing since 1825 and is truly magnificent. This was the first official social function to honor Nathalie and me and it was held at noon on New Year's Day, 2002.

During the second week in January, I held a meeting at Oak Hill Middle School to introduce my philosophy to all city employees. I wanted the public to get to know my plans for the city. Over 100 people came and were introduced to and got to know Danny Brown, whom I had appointed as interim personnel manager, to speak.

In creating a re-organizational group to re-structure Milledgeville's government, I named former police chief Fred Hayes as interim Director of the city's code enforcement and public works department; Barry Jarrett as City, Water and Sewerage Director; Sherrie Whittington as City Finance Director and Danny Brown as the new City Personnel Director. I decided that Hayes should be coordinator of the group because he had experience as a former city manager and because he was planning to leave Milledgeville. He had no biases ruling his decisions and he knew what had to be done. The group's task was a big one: they were to review each department and find ways to increase effectiveness so that each department would be working at maximum efficiency. Ideally, they would review each city department — city marshal's office, water and sewerage, fire department, police department, personnel, and the finance and clerk's office — and have suggestions for improvement by April 1, 2002. I was very interested in seeing what they would do and planned on taking their suggestions to City Council.

My First City Council Meeting

Our first city council meeting was held on January 8, 2002. We had a lot to do in this meeting and I wanted to go ahead and make some initial changes in the way the city was run. Two immediate changes were the additions of a chaplain and a student at the council meeting each month. The chaplain would be selected from a different district each month and would be on call for the entire month in the event that a member of the clergy was needed. A different student would attend each month to lead the Pledge of Allegiance. It is my firm belief that if we expect the young people in our communities to be effective leaders some day, then they need to witness the process in action.

During that first meeting, we awarded former mayor Johnny Grant with a plaque and gavel for his years of service to the city of Milledgeville. Despite the fact that I felt he was an ineffective mayor, he *had* put in 24 years of his life. I appointed Jeanette Walden as mayor pro tern, the position held by Dennette Jackson, another council member and I scheduled our first "open dialogue" night, the first of what I hoped would be monthly events in which the public was invited to come and share their concerns about city issues, make suggestions, and hear about what was going on with the running of the city. Perhaps the biggest change of the evening was the issue of committees. Rather than have all these small committees running around with a lengthy chain of command, I proposed that the council meet as one large committee to handle the business. I proposed this for an indefinite period of time. Alderman Jeanette Walden put forth the motion and Dennette Jackson seconded, but Richard Mullins put forth a substitute motion that the proposal only last for 90 days. I had hoped that the council would have enough trust in me to move the city forward that the proposal would pass. However, the trial period proposal passed with a vote of 4-2. I wanted to start off my tenure as mayor by working *with* council, not at odds with them, but this was not to be. We also planned our first "dialogue night" for 7pm on January 29th at Oak Hill Middle School.

Martin Luther King Day fell on January 22 in 2002 and I'm proud to say that I was Honorary Grand Marshall for the day in Atlanta. Milledgeville had several events planned for the day, the first of which was a street party in his honor from 10am until 3pm. At 5pm, we marched from Central City Park to Flagg Chapel Baptist Church where Rev. Omar Reid was the pastor. I was the key note speaker at the church after the march ended. I was pleased that both black and white to came out to hear what I had to say. The civil rights movement wasn't a "black" thing. Plenty of whites were injured and killed fighting for the equality of all people. I think a lot of people are ignorant of that fact and it adversely colors their view of the civil rights movement. Nathalie and I had marched with Dr. King and other great leaders in Montgomery and I had the opportunity to meet and talk with him. Martin Luther King and the movement gave me hope and the vision that America would change one day. And that a Floyd Griffin could be a senator and a mayor; that I could be anything I wanted to be. Based on all that I had experienced as part of Dr. King's movement while I was a student activist, I knew could achieve anything. He had a major impact on me; on who I am today and what I stand for.

Our first "dialogue night" arrived. Taped by Georgia College and State University to be broadcast later on television and attended by about 170 people, I thought it went pretty good. In order to show unity between myself and City Council, questions were directed to the specific department heads that would handle those affairs. This was also an excellent way to get the public acquainted with the appointees. To be fair, several citizens had some very legitimate questions and concerns and I answered them honestly and frankly.

One audience member was concerned about the possible misuse of our special purpose sales tax funds. I understood his concern; Sherrie Whittington (the new city clerk and treasurer) and I had discovered that about $70,000 in SPLOST money had been included in the city's general budget. I assured the gentleman that the money had already been put into a special separate account to be used only for that purpose. We also assured the audience that there would now be a quarterly budget review to ensure that all monies would be handled honestly and appropriately. The city had a budget deficit of over a million dollars and I announced that I had instituted a hiring freeze and that no major purchases would be made until we could get the budget under control. At the time, I was looking into ways to bring money in without having to raise any taxes.

Other questions centered on city services, the hiring of a city manager, possible city-county consolidation, and City Council unity. Overall, I felt that it was a very successful night. Certainly, the citizens that were present would begin to realize that I was serious about wanting to know their concerns and about hearing any suggestions they might have.

Unfortunately, the format I introduced of "committee as a whole" meetings didn't last long. At our council meeting on February 12th, I went back to the original setup of having standing committees headed by council members. I did this because several council members had approached me and stated that they felt left out of city business with the new format. I did, however, appoint "committees of one" to oversee city department business. These individuals were subcommittees intended to oversee business for the duration of the 90-day trial period that we would have the council sit as a whole. The committees of one that I appointed at this council meeting were Richard Mullins to Personnel; Dennette Jackson to water and sewerage; Ken Vance to public works; Denise Shinholster to clerk and finance; Richard Hudson to the fire department; and Jeanette Walden to law enforcement. I appointed myself as chairman of the committee that was to begin looking at the process of dividing the local option sales tax between the city and Baldwin County. I also had Ken Vance and Sherri Whittington on that committee with me. We also addressed the annexation of "islands" within the city limits. Richard Hudson, Jeanette Walden, and Denise Shinholster were to look at these annexations.

On February 21, I gave a speech at Georgia College & State University. I have always appreciated the opportunity to speak to young people because I believe that this is where our future lies. On discussing Black History Month, I spoke to a future where blacks would not rely on one month of the year to recognize our heroes. The potential for this is in our educated youth. I called for the students to be beacons of hope to others, not just a result of affirmative action. It takes that little extra something to be successful; you have to do more than just come to the table. You have to be willing to go the extra mile, not just for yourself, but for those who will surely follow you.

My first obvious power struggle with city council occurred in March. This concerned our contract with Sinclair Disposal Service to pick up our garbage. There were some errors in the wording of the contract and I absolutely refused to sign a contract that had the potential for a lot of later problems. So I vetoed the resolution to extend the contract with SDS. City Council promptly overrode my veto by a vote of 5-1. I just could not understand this. Actually, Denise Shinholster was right when she addressed city attorney J.W. Morgan about not speaking up on errors in the contract. This should have been done before it went in front of city council. But it wasn't and I wasn't backing down. In this one incident, I could see where a different mayor just going along placidly would set the stage for a lot of nothing happening. It would just be riding along on a sea of inefficiency, when the whole point of my becoming mayor was to see a future of improvement. This meant improvement in *all* areas. Why not start improving right here? Unfortunately, council didn't see it that way. I suppose they were content to just ride along with things the way they were. I wasn't. In any event, I declared the current contract with SDS as void because of the way it was written and Morgan (city attorney) began negotiations with SDS to produce a new contract.

Another example of the council's sometimes odd decision-making was its approval, later in March 2002, by a vote of 5-1, of the SDS contract for garbage pickup, despite the contract's flaws. I signed the contract because council approved the amendments I put forth, including the stipulation that the contract could not be extended without going through the bidding process. However, because of an extension clause in the contract, Council was able to extend the contract (which would expire in May) without bidding, despite the fact that the city charter requires bidding on any contracts over $5,000. I didn't feel good about this one, but there was nothing I could do about it. Surprisingly, Councilman Ken Vance agreed with me on this one, casting the one dissenting vote.

Soon after, I also asked city council to approve hiring an outside company, Governmental Solutions, to analyze and give us an evaluation on the current distribution between the city and Baldwin County of the local option sales tax, at a cost of no more than $29,000. The council agreed with me by a vote of 4-2. I believe the council's decision to back me on this issue was facilitated by the presence at these meetings of Alfred Outland III, director of policy and communications for the Georgia Municipal Association. He was good enough to come in and explain to everyone exactly what LOST was and how the funds are normally distributed. This was quite a chunk of money we were talking about and I felt that we should be on top of what was going on from the outset.

During the April 23rd council meeting, I appointed the city council members to committees, as follows: Dennette Jackson as chair of the personnel and ethics committee and vice chair of water and sewer; Jeanette Walden as chair of the finance committee and vice chair of physical properties; Denise Shinholster as chair of public safety and vice chair of personnel and ethics and finance committees; Ken Vance as chair of public works/governmental affairs and water and sewer committees; Richard Mullins as vice chair of public works/ governmental affairs; and Richard Hudson as chair of the physical properties committee and vice chair of public safety. I also introduced resolution to appoint department heads of several city offices, that is, to keep on everyone that was already serving in those capacities. This was passed on to the personnel and ethics committee for review. During this same council meeting, I introduced resolution to amend the city's operating budget, increasing everyone's salaries except the marshal's office, which was decreased by over $49,000. I passed this resolution on to the finance committee for consideration.

Trouble with City Council

By the beginning of April 2002, it became apparent that there was no unity between me and the Milledgeville City Council. One particular council meeting stands out in my mind as evidence of this fact. This meeting had been called to address accusations from several members of council who charged that I had not been forthright with my plans to reorganize the city government or with my proposal to shift $62,000 of the budget changes. I never understood this—my plans for Milledgeville had never been a secret. One needed only to ask—or rather, just listen—when these plans were discussed. It probably didn't help relations when Beverly Calhoun stood up during the meeting to question the council about its lack of support for my vision of the city's future. Mrs. Calhoun singled out Denise Shinholster and Richard Mullins as the focus of her concerns. Then the mud really started to fly.

All but one council member insisted to the press afterwards that I must have put Mrs. Calhoun up to her actions, a suggestion I still find ludicrous. I have never felt the need to have someone defend me or my actions; I believe Mrs. Calhoun was merely voicing a concern about the obvious lack of unity between me and city council. To his credit, City Councilman Ken Vance told the press that although he thought Mrs. Calhoun's remarks were inappropriate, he had never had a problem communicating with me and didn't understand why everyone else did.

Relations were strained even further at the May 28th city council meeting. Councilman Richard Hudson had a big surprise for me in the form of six resolutions to rescind several of my previous actions. The first resolution called for the rules of order to be suspended so that his other five resolutions could pass with enough votes that night, without being sent back to any committees and without a second reading. One of the resolutions called for council meetings to be conducted as stated in the city charter (rescinding the 90-day temporary "council as a whole" meetings), and a second resolution offered the notion that "except for those duties expressly conferred on the Mayor, there is no reference to the issuance of Executive Orders," resolving that three executive orders I had enacted earlier in the month would be rescinded. Councilman Vance, who abstained from voting on the resolutions, was very vocal about how he felt about the matter. "I didn't know about this until a little while ago," he said. "I'm not prepared for this and I don't like to be unprepared....I don't appreciate not having a chance to do my homework and making me look like I look right now," he told his peers.

I was glad that the cameras weren't rolling during that meeting because the proceedings were an example of the political process at its worst. I announced my intention to veto every bit of it, and on June 4, I did just that. I vetoed the resolution that city-council meetings be held as outlined in the city charter, because of the implication that I had done otherwise. I regret the fact that the council had a problem with the parliamentary procedure I was trying to implement and did not come to me to discuss it. As far as the issuance of executive orders is concerned, I vetoed this resolution because I had issued executive orders, as opposed to oral or written directives, as a means to document my actions for future reference. I did this for everyone's good, so that there would be written documentation of every action I took. Every veto of every resolution was done upon advice of the city attorney.

These incidents let me know, in no uncertain terms, what I was dealing with. Most of City Council seemed to want to disagree with every resolution and plan that I came up with, almost as a matter of course. Whether or not the council members understood what they were voting against didn't seem to matter to them, as long as they voted against me. This type of petty behavior was displayed for all the public to see in August when Shinholster and Hudson made remarks to the press, saying (in the words of a concerned citizen who wrote to the local newspaper to complain), "If you don't let me play with your ball, I won't play with you." Hudson was quoted as saying, "Even if an idea from the mayor sounds good, the council will decline it to get their message across." I knew that this kind of atmosphere was going to make any kind of progress for Milledgeville difficult, if not impossible. But I was determined to do what I was elected to do, and that was to move Milledgeville to the next level.

Reflections From Nathalie

The powers that be in this city were fighting, tooth and nail, to keep things the way they have always been. And when you get a progressive mayor, this is one of the challenges he's going to face. That was the thing with Floyd. People were constantly trying to tell him how to run the city. Part of the problem was a basic lack of respect. Most of the resistance Floyd received as mayor would not have happened if people respected one another and the talents that they bring to office. But this is something that has to be learned young—people need to teach their children to have proper respect. They need to teach them about the Civil Rights Movement, because many kids nowadays don't know about their history and what others went through in order for them to have the opportunities they often take for granted.

Instead of encountering a spirit of cooperation and compromise, he was greeted with skepticism, criticism, and in some cases outright hostility by those who were in power. We must recognize that there is comfort in familiarity, therefore when someone or something comes along to challenge or threaten that comfort zone, people react defensively. That is how I view Milledgeville. Even today, it is a city where few want to change the way things have always been done because it intrudes on their comfort zone.

Thankfully, I've had Floyd all these years to help me cope with the small-minded nature of some people. He is a very dedicated person. Very focused. His parents were very influential in helping him achieve many of his goals. I think he's a dreamer, too, but not the head-in-the-clouds type; he thinks of things that can be productive—I'm just the opposite. But Floyd has always had a vision of what life could be, and when we moved back to Milledgeville after retiring, he wanted to pursue that kind of life.

He and I thought things would be different when we came back in 1990 because we had lived in so many places and seen how the world had changed for the better, as it relates to race relations and opportunities. However, that kind of progress had not yet fully affected our hometown at the time of our return.

Yet, in spite of all of the barriers that were placed in his path, in spite of all of the questionable negative press, in spite of all of the "behind closed door" politics, Floyd did impact his community in positive ways and I truly believe that one day his term in office will be viewed as a missed opportunity.

PLEASANT MOMENTS IN THE MIDST OF BATTLE

In June of 2002, the city honored a great man after his passing on May 30 of that year. Lt. David Kendrick had been employed with the Milledgeville Police Department for more than 29 years, retiring in 1993. He had also worked at Central State Hospital for 34 years before retiring in 1999. City Council and I presented Kendrick's family with a resolution honoring him for his service to the city. As one of the first African Americans to serve on the Milledgeville police force, along with Herman Rozier, Kendrick made history and helped to shape the city of Milledgeville. Not only that, he was a good guy.

City Hall was packed the night we honored Kendrick. Chief Woodrow Blue, Lt. Bobby Cheeves, and Chief of Detectives Mark Bell, III, were joined by others whose lives David had touched and changed. Councilman Ken Vance, who had known him for many years, was right on the mark with the comments he made about Kendrick at the ceremony. "We could be here awhile if we start telling David Kendrick stories," said Vance. "I worked closely with him as a law-enforcement officer....You knew, when you called, that David was coming. He did his job and he took care of his family. You just had to know him. He wasn't very loud; you'd look up and he'd just be there." All in all, it was a moving celebration of Kendrick's life. I was very proud that the city officials, despite our differences, had come together to do this for Kendrick's family.

During the weekend of June 22, I got a brief but much-needed break from the Milledgeville City Council. I headed to Washington, D.C., having been chosen as part of a delegation representing the state of Georgia in a fellowship program at George Washington University. Georgia's Department of Industry, Trade, and Tourism invited me to represent the state at the Elliott School of International Affairs in a program entitled "Governing in the Global Age." I was joined by senior members of the executive and legislative branches of government, as well as by senior educators and business leaders. This event allowed me to meet and have dialogue about globalization with leaders from all over the country.

Misunderstood by many, "globalization" simply means that the world is growing smaller, a fact that has an effect on many facets of everyday living. For example, today's youth can talk to others their age in practically any other country in the world, and immigration is bridging and merging cultures as never before. The conference encouraged attendees to examine the ramifications of globalization and use these to our benefit. I was especially interested in the matter of immigrants, for many had settled in the Milledgeville area, with English as their second language. The event in Washington lasted several days and included discussions about security, jobs, wages, education, and other issues.

The Milledgeville City Council headed to Savannah to attend the annual GMA (Georgia Municipal Association) Convention. This is a yearly training weekend during which council members attend classes all day on Saturday, and then attend meetings on different items of interest on the following three days. Members get to meet and share ideas with politicians from other districts.

About this time, Council approved my choices for city department heads. They did not like my choice of Barry Jarrett for Public Works and, in fact, approved him as Water and Sewer director by a narrow margin, but everyone else was approved unanimously. Jerome

"Tom" Dietrich was confirmed as fire chief, Woodrow Blue as chief of police, Sherrie Leverette as clerk and treasurer, and Danny Brown as personnel director.

Another bright spot during this period was the fact that council agreed to budget $29,000 to hire Governmental Solutions to analyze and evaluate the Baldwin County current sales-tax distribution. But during the following months, the bright spot turned into a blemish as the city and county governments engaged in a tug-of-war over the division of the tax revenue. This was an important issue because it would determine what percentage of LOST (local option sales tax) revenue the city of Milledgeville would receive and what percentage would go to Baldwin County. This distribution is reevaluated every ten years at the time of the census and is generally based on population. At the time, the city was receiving 39 percent of some ten million dollars generated annually by the tax in Baldwin County. Our population percentage had grown by about 2 percent since the last census, which meant that if we could negotiate our portion of the tax to an increase of 2 percent, it would mean an additional $200,000 a year or two million dollars over the next ten years.

Negotiations began in earnest in July and, as it turned out, the county's first proposal concerning LOST was completely unacceptable. Baldwin County first proposed 69 percent for them and 31 percent for us. If we had accepted this first proposal, it would have put a tremendous strain on the city's finances, which were already in the red. We had requested 45 percent, leaving the county with 55 percent. I felt that this was a fair starting point for negotiations. It wasn't lost on me or on the city-council members that the county, with its original proposal of a 69/31 split, seemed to think that it could appear magnanimous with acceptance of any less of a percentage in further negotiations. We counter-proposed 43.5 percent of the first $5.2 million collected (56.5 percent to the county), and 30 percent of the surplus collected over that amount (with 70 percent going to the county).

Over the next couple of months, several proposals were made by the county, none of which were acceptable. By October, it was evident that outside arbitration would be needed to settle the matter. Now we had to decide who would arbitrate. The county suggested that the city and county each choose an arbiter. Each of the two arbiters would then choose a third, with all of them coming from the community. I wasn't crazy about the idea; with this much at stake, I preferred hiring professionals. But I opted to wait and see what the county's next move would be. In any event, the city and the county would have to come to an agreement before December 31, 2002, or the revenue would be lost to both governments. As it turned out, negotiations continued until December, when County Commissioner Bobby Blizzard (head of the county's LOST negotiations committee) and I asked State Representative Bobby Parham to step in and serve as mediator. It took him about ten minutes to resolve the issue by convincing me and everyone else on both sides to leave everything as it had been for the last ten years. And that was that.

July 8, 2002 was a special day for the city of Milledgeville and I couldn't possibly write this book without including this event. Several weeks before that date, I had contacted Rene Ferge Marty, the French consul general, to discuss the possibility of forging a sister-city relationship with an area of France that resembled Milledgeville economically and educationally. Whenever this has been done elsewhere, it has opened the door for student-exchange programs, diplomatic travel, and economic and trade opportunities. A partnership also carries the benefits of engaging in a wide array of activities, including business, municipal, professional, and cultural projects.

What I proposed had happened once before in our city's history. In 1825, the Marquis de Lafayette and his dog Quiz spent a few days at the governor's mansion in Milledgeville, because at that time, it was the state capital. Lafayette was a hero of the American Revolution, a military officer and advisor during the time when America was being founded. He had "adopted" our country, contributing to the pro-American sentiment in France and to the signing of a treaty of alliance with the colonies in 1778. Until his death in 1834, he worked to secure commercial concessions for our country and was one of the most powerful men of his time.

So it should come as no surprise that city officials and other residents were excited when the French consul general agreed to the idea and planned a visit with us. We really rolled out the red carpet for Marty's arrival. Our day began with breakfast at the Antebellum Inn, a bed & breakfast, where we were joined by Barrow Tabet, former president of the International Club at Baldwin High School. This was followed by a walking tour of Main Street, a tour of the Old Capitol Building, and lunch at the Hoke Dining Hall at Georgia State College & University. Marty spoke during the luncheon, saying, "It is with great welcome that I accept your hospitality. It is a day fit for a king…I cannot thank you enough for your very warm welcome." At 3 p.m., Marty attended our city council meeting, during which we declared July 8th as Consul General Rene Ferge Marty Day. The day was an absolute success, with Marty declaring he would travel to Paris on July 15 and suggest to French officials that a relationship be formed between Milledgeville and a region in the Southwest portion of France where Marty had lived for two years.

During the July 31 council meeting, I proposed a resolution to change the end of our fiscal year from December 31 to June 30. I expected the typical grumbling and dissent that I was fast becoming accustomed to, but I was pleasantly surprised when the council seemed to favor the proposal. Most of this acceptance, I believe, was due to the fact that clerk and treasurer Sherrie Leverette was in favor of the resolution. She astutely realized that the change would ease the city's financial burden and create an easier workload for her office staff. "We would have money in the middle of the year," she said. "The money would be coming in the first and second quarters, rather than the last quarters." Leverette added, "Rather than having all of our accounting year-ends and our payroll year-ends both coming on December 31st, that would split our workload." She went on to explain to council that payroll and salary could continue to be done on December 31 and that the rest of the accounting year-end would fall on June 30. I pointed out that if we accepted the proposal, we would no longer have to work on a budget during an election year and that the incoming administration would not have to function off of the last administration's budget. At the following meeting, Councilman Ken Vance made a motion to send the resolution to full council for consideration. Vance recognized that the fiscal-year change would put us in line to receive grants from the state. He said, "It makes grants easier. It makes business with the state easier, because everybody else that does business with us operates on this fiscal year." Council finally accepted the fiscal year change.

Around the first of August, I was appointed to the Georgia Municipal Association's Youth Leadership Task Force. This organization fit in with my firm belief that our youth should become more interested in and educated about the civic life of their communities. I really wanted to see our young people get more involved in volunteer work at our area hospitals, churches, and nursing homes. Appointment to this task force seemed a great way to move in that direction. Georgia Municipal Association (GMA) president and Mayor of Savannah Floyd Adams appointed me, telling a reporter, "The GMA Task Force is geared to stimulate young people's interest in public service....I'm delighted that Mayor Griffin has agreed to serve on this task force and be a guide in developing this program." I knew that through this task force, I could generate new ideas for our local youth and would have the benefit of receiving input from other mayors and leaders from around the state.

When I became aware that a state history museum was in the works and that its location had not yet been determined, I wrote a letter on August 20 to Cathy Cox, who was, at the time, Georgia's Secretary of State. In this letter, I recommended Milledgeville as the ideal site for the new museum. In fact, at the risk of sounding biased, I can say that I couldn't think of a better location in all the state than Milledgeville. We have a rich history full of the intrigue and turbulence of the South's past, not to mention the fact that Milledgeville was the first city in the state to serve as the capital. In my letter, I mentioned the historical landmarks Milledgeville already possessed, such as the newly restored Old State Capitol building, the Old Governor's Mansion, and Memory Hill Cemetery. I pointed out that the city is located near the center of the state and major highways 441 and 22/24, which handle considerable traffic flow, and that it has an abundance of accommodations and restaurants that could easily handle tourists. I was pleased to quickly receive a response from Cathy on August 29. "We, too, are excited about this possibility," she wrote. "We have just reached the stage of beginning discussions about the most appropriate location for a museum and would most certainly put Milledgeville on the table for discussion." Cathy felt like the historic treasures Milledgeville already possessed would make it a desirable location. I immediately started organizing a committee of educational and political leaders to follow up on this unique and rare opportunity.

Atlanta seemed to be our biggest competition for the location of the museum. Chamber of Commerce president Tara Peters, in charge of leading the effort to get the museum located in Milledgeville, did an awesome job leading the committee in gathering the information we needed for a promotional packet that would be sent to selection-committee members, legislators, and any others across the state who might support Milledgeville as the best location. The proposal packet carried the slogan *Milledgeville: Another Capital Idea* and included a map showing the city's prime location in the state, its current historic attractions, and the proposed site for the museum, complete with parking outlines. "This promotional packet will hopefully sway the selection committee to choose Milledgeville all the way," wrote Peters.

During the week prior to September 11, 2002, city council and I asked the public to honor those that had fallen in the terrorist attacks the previous year by observing, on the morning of the 11th, a moment of silence at 8:48, the time that the first plane hit the World Trade Center. The citizens complied. American flags all over town flew half-mast at the designated time in remembrance of those that had lost their lives.

Around this time, City Council introduced a resolution to change the form of government from a mayor-council setup to that of city manager-council. I would have to conclude that this was done to take away what little power I had. Of course, I immediately vetoed the resolution. The city had operated successfully on the mayor-council form of government for 199 years and I saw no reason to change that. I told Council that we would just have to learn to work together. They then got together and, at the next meeting, voted unanimously to override my veto. I didn't understand this aggressive move by Council to push ahead with the idea. But I wasn't going to give in without a fight. At the very least, I wanted the citizens' views on what type of government they wanted to see working for Milledgeville. Council wanted me to approve this resolution without a thought about public opinion; I felt it was something that needed careful thought and consideration. I foresaw that this difference of opinion between me and the council members would follow us into the New Year.

Bicentennial

During the February 26, 2002 council meeting, I appointed a 26-member committee to oversee the planning of all events for Milledgeville's 200th birthday, coming up in 2003. Our Bicentennial was an important part of our city's history and I wanted our citizens to take part in a variety of events to celebrate this landmark in history. City and community pride are an integral part of unity, thus everyone should participate in one form or another. I felt that Jane Sowell, Executive Director of the Milledgeville-Baldwin County Convention and Visitor's Center, would be the perfect person to lead the effort. The committee also included Nathalie and E.G. Baugh (wife of a former mayor) as co-chairs, current and past members of city government, and various community members. We wanted to make sure that the committee accurately represented the city of Milledgeville, thus we had blacks, whites and Hispanics, as well as members from the various economic groups of the city.

Two hundred years ago in 1802, working under the direction of President Thomas Jefferson, four men signed a treaty with the Creek Indians for a tract of land west of the Oconee River. By the following year, Milledgeville and Baldwin County had been founded. According to Bob Wilson, a history professor at Georgia College & State University, Milledgeville remains one of the few cities in the country that was laid out intentionally as a capital, being designated thus as Georgia's capital in 1804. The statehouse, now Georgia Military College, was built on the eastern side of the city near the Oconee River and Washington Street, and was meant to run between this statehouse and the governor's mansion — just like Washington DC. But the land was swampy and low-lying and the mansion had to be built two blocks away, on the western side of the city. Georgia College was actually the site of Milledgeville's first prison and on the southern end of town sits Memory Hill Cemetery, originally a public square for schools and churches. When only one church built there and then moved, Memory

Hill became the primary cemetery and eventually, a landmark. As I've often said, Milledgeville is rich in history; one need only spend the day with us to be taken back to another time.

By the beginning of 2003, almost everyone in Milledgeville had started getting excited about our Bicentennial. We held a kick-off party on Saturday, January 18 at Russell Auditorium on the campus of Georgia College and State University. Jane Sowell credited Lynda Banks and Natalie Goodrich with a successful day. "I've been waiting to birth this baby for a year," Sowell said. "I think it went well." That was an understatement; the day was fantastic. Bob Wilson made the opening remarks of the day, saying "Milledgeville is celebrating its journey down a path still shaped in deep and profound ways by the fact that for 61 years, we were the state capital." Well said, professor. I gave a short speech, as did Baldwin County Commission Chairman Ace Parker, and a group of Georgia College students gave a re-enactment of the treaty signing. One highlight of the day was when the Baldwin County High School band played a rousing rendition of a John Philip Sousa march, complete with drum solos. For the first event of the year-long Bicentennial Celebration, it was a wonderful start.

In February, I led a delegation of Milledgeville residents to the Capitol in Atlanta where we received formal recognition for our Bicentennial. At the previous Tuesday's council meeting, I invited the public to join us and to my pleasant surprise, many did. Several officials and civic leaders also went, including Tara Peters, president and CEO of the Milledgeville/Baldwin County Chamber of Commerce. "The mayor had some very nice words to say about Milledgeville and it was important that we got our name out there today," she said. "We do have quite a significant ceremony coming up and it was important for the legislature to see us." Milledgeville's Bicentennial was recognized with resolutions from the House and the Senate. These resolutions merely energized an already excited city about the events coming up all year long.

In May, we honored Memory Hill Cemetery's bicentennial with an impressive gathering of speakers and music. The Bicentennial Legacy Committee, chaired by Ms. Florida Gardner and Ms. Lorene Flanders, sponsored the event that brought more than 100 people to sit in the shade and celebrate our history. The Trinity CME Adult Choir started off the day, followed by Ms. Gardner's description of just what the Bicentennial Legacy does. "Our objective is to create, extend, and move forward activities to the city that can be passed on to future generations to enrich their lives," she explained. Ms. Flanders then gave a short history of the cemetery, detailing how its story is intertwined with that of three local churches; how it was first called "the graveyard," then "the cemetery," then its first reference as "Memory Hill" in 1945 in a newspaper article. She also noted that the cemetery is on the National Register of Historic places, as demonstrated by the plaque on the front gates.

Just inside the front gates of Memory Hill is a gazebo where new storyboards have been constructed and placed to tell about the people and events that helped shape this historic site. Dr. Kathy Fuller, chair of the Memory Hill Cemetery subgroup of the Bicentennial Legacy Committee, spoke about these storyboards to the crowd. "We wanted to tie Memory Hill to significant events in the community and Georgia," she said. "We hope to illustrate that those who rest here continue to influence our lives."

With July came our *July-Fest,* a combination of Independence Day and our bicentennial — our 200th Fourth of July! The festival was held at Walter B. Williams Recreation Center and held a myriad of activities for all ages. The parking lot was filled with vendors selling all the traditional July 4th delights — hotdogs, hamburgers, fries and sodas. But the real fun kicked in at 5:30pm when the City versus County softball game started. For what was supposed to be a "fun" game, the competition was fierce. In the first game, the County spanked us good with a final score of 16-1, but we got serious in the second game, beating the county with a score of 13-8. In an unusual turn of events, city council members and I got along just fine. Somehow, we set aside our differences for the day and the overall mood was relaxed; the camaraderie was good.

The Police Department brought along their color guard and the Fire Department put on a great fireworks display that evening. All day long, children ran around, screamed, and played games of chase, until by fireworks time, most were completely worn out. Thinking back, the day seems almost surreal, something right out of a Norman Rockwell painting. It was one of those days that just seems to burn itself into your memory; something to look back on and smile about.

The culmination of the celebration of the Milledgeville Bicentennial took place on On December 11, 2003. We ended a very successful yearlong celebration by dedicating the new Black Heritage Plaza. The project began during the summer as the McIntosh Street Project, following a $65,000 grant approval from the Knight Foundation. Randy Cannon, Allied Arts director, was excited about the dedication, and with good reason. The park had turned out beautifully, sporting a monument dedicated to the African Americans who had owned successful businesses in that block of town, and also featuring a stage where artists and performers could hold events.

The ceremony began with performances by D'Vine, a gospel group from Atlanta that has performed all over the world. We then officially dedicated the plaza and unveiled the monument, concluding the ceremony with more music by D'Vine. The public had the opportunity to make a lasting contribution to the park by purchasing a bench for a price close to $1,000. The benches would include engravings of the buyers' names. The event turned out to be a truly nice ceremony with a good turnout of citizens, and I was proud of the effort and work that Randy Cannon had put into making a vision of mine become a reality.

Chapter 10

2003 in Office

The last order of business for the year 2002 was adjusting the 2002 budget and passing the one for 2003. These meetings went smoothly and consisted mainly of shifting in line item money around in order to balance the accounts. Obviously we had overspent at times due to the very tight budget the city was on because of the large deficit. Everyone agreed on the actions because it was the thing to do – we were simply taking care of the city's business.

Despite the debate over the form of government Milledgeville should have and the ludicrous back-and-forth about the Sinclair Disposal Systems' $2 million contract, I was able to achieve some progress for the city during the year. In January of 2002, I had promised to attract new business to the city and this promise was realized when, mid-year, we saw Lowe's and WalMart choose Milledgeville as the location for new stores. Our water line expansion project moved forward with new lines completed throughout the county. We also discovered about $400,000 in unpaid water bills and we promptly passed a tougher water bill payment deadline and added a disconnection process.

Thus, I felt some pride in the accomplishments that were achieved the previous year. But this feeling was tempered by the knowledge that the upcoming year would be an uphill battle for nearly anything that I hoped to do.

I gave my State of the City address on Tuesday, January 14th, at our first city council meeting of the year. I had four specific goals for the year 2003. They were: Improving the quality of life for Milledgeville's citizens; making Milledgeville a more effective and efficient government; working closely with various partners to improve economic development; and initiating a study to consider the feasibility of consolidating city and county governments. I also requested a grant to aid with the Bicentennial plans and pledged to work with local and state officials in an effort to secure Milledgeville as the location of the new Georgia State History Museum. The following year would see only partial success in these goals.

I regained some hope for the upcoming year with one of the first orders of business for city council. During our January 8th council meeting, Developer Miles Hill of Charter Companies spoke to us, asking us to approve an elderly housing apartment complex for Milledgeville. The Department of Community Affairs had denied them the tax credits needed for this endeavor two years before and they were making a second attempt. I favored the idea because Milledgeville had a fairly substantial elderly community that was not to the point of needing assisted living. I was somewhat worried over council's response to this because Charter Companies needed 7% of the operating costs for the first 10 years from the city of Milledgeville. I was pleasantly surprised however, when council approved the resolution unanimously.

January 20th saw the biggest ever celebration of Martin Luther King, Jr.'s birthday as the Southern Christian Leadership Conference gathered at Flagg Chapel Baptist where the Rev. Omer Reid is pastor. Beginning at Central City Park, over 250 people marched to the Baldwin County Courthouse carrying signs with messages like "Keep the dream alive – January 20, 2003" and "Celebrate King's dream and your dream." After arriving at the courthouse, the marchers and others gathered to hear several people speak, myself included. Blacks had come a long way in my generation, but people need to remember Dr. King and what he stood for. Your average young person, if he/she even knows who King was, doesn't know what he stood for and what he died for.

Once the speakers had finished at the courthouse, everyone marched several more blocks to Flagg Chapel where the guest speaker was Rev. Tony Fraley of Spring Hill Baptist Church. "We've been fighting for a long time," said Rev. Fraley. The fight, in some ways, is just getting started. Dr. King and other civil rights leaders fought for this…..any person who does not know their history is bound to repeat it. I don't want to go back and I don't want our children to go back," he concluded.

The Second Macedonia Baptist Church male chorus, the County Line Baptist Church Choir, and dance groups from Wesley Chapel AME Church all performed in celebration of King's birthday. People of every race held hands and hummed the tune of "Lift Every Voice and Sing" while Leann Hightower read King's famous speech "I Have a Dream." This was one of the most moving of my days as mayor of Milledgeville. It's difficult not to pay tribute to someone who died for your rights and freedoms, and to see so many different people join together in this tribute made me want to work even harder to help realize some of King's dreams for our city.

In April, I was compelled to ask the GBI to look into allegations that councilman Richard Mullins had made death threats toward me to a local grocery store employee. The threat was told to Beverly Calhoun, a friend of mine, and she brought it to my attention. When I asked the employee if it was true, he told me that Mullins had said to him, "I ought to give you a gun so you can shoot Griffin." Despite the trouble between city council and me, I still felt that this was way over the line, so I asked the GBI to investigate. Apparently, they felt that it was a serious matter as well; they began a preliminary investigation. Of course, Mullins said it was a lie. The GBI investigated, but were unable to find any proof with which to prosecute Mullins, so they dropped the case. I mention this incident because it was one of several and it demonstrates a little of what I was going through at the time.

In May, I received a wonderful surprise that really lifted my spirits and helped me renew my efforts to lead Milledgeville to new heights. The HistoryMakers, a Chicago-based organization dedicated to recognizing leading African Americans in their chosen fields, decided to honor me as one of only two hundred individuals from all over the country. I traveled to Chicago and stayed for two days and it was one of the most wonderful experiences of my life. I was able to talk to other honorees from all walks of life about Milledgeville and our upcoming Bicentennial. For example, Cleo Robinson, a dancer from Denver, CO who owns a dance company, offered to come to Milledgeville to have a performance and work with our young people. James Curtis, an anchor with Court TV, also expressed an interest in coming here to work with the youth of Milledgeville.

The organization videotaped an extensive interview with me about my entire life and they sent me home with a beautiful bronze statue. It was just an awesome experience and I was humbled to have been chosen along with such leaders, individuals at the top of their professions.

The month of June also had great things in store for me. The Georgia Conference of Black Mayors chose to elect me as their next president, following Mayor C. Jack Ellis of Macon. The GCBM is actually a subsidiary of the National Conference of Black Mayors, based in Atlanta and consisting of a membership of more than 500 black mayors all over the country. This group is a non-profit organization that provides the country's black mayors with technical support and management assistance as well as lobbying for our concerns on a national level. The Georgia Conference has a membership of over 30 mayors from across the state, serving cities as large as Atlanta and as small as 500 residents.

The GCBM usually meets quarterly and our first meeting with me serving as president would be held sometime in August here in Milledgeville. One of my goals as president was to identify federal and state funds that could help us better serve our cities. I considered it a great honor to be elected to this position and saw it as a way for all of Milledgeville to benefit from the exposure our city would gain from my experience.

Also around mid-year, Allied Arts Director Randy Cannon appeared before the city council to ask permission to begin work on the $65,000 "McIntosh Street Project." Last year, I had asked Randy to apply to the Knight Foundation for the money to build a small park in the center of town to honor where many African Americans had owned businesses and done their shopping decades before. Last December, the foundation contacted Randy and assured him that they would indeed fund the project. This was great news and the physical properties committee voted unanimously to approve Randy's request. Plans for the park included a small stage for concerts, walkways, and greenspace surrounding the area. A local committee was also set up to design a monument to place in the park. Randy was very excited and plans immediately got under way. "Toole Engineering was selected to design the space. We received bids from several companies, but they were the most competitive and because of their knowledge of the Streetscape project, it made a great deal of sense to use them," he said. I requested that the park be completed by October 18th and Randy worked very hard to make that possible.

On September 11, the city held a special ceremony inside Hatcher Square Mall to remember those who had lost their lives two years earlier in the terrorist attacks on the World Trade Center twin towers, the Pentagon, and the plane crash in Pennsylvania. When I spoke, I pointed out that the attacks had resulted in a higher level of police presence at places and events that are possible terrorist targets. Georgia Military College president Peter Boylan pointed out that the attacks brought America closer together. "I think there are a number of moments in American life that really define America," he said. "There are some that are still mentioned today – Pearl Harbor, the assassination of John F. Kennedy, the assassination of Martin Luther King. Nine-eleven is one of those defining moments in American history," he concluded.

12 year-old Chay Aycock, a seventh grade cadet at GMC, ended the ceremony beautifully with her rendition of "America the Beautiful."

That day, we also dedicated a brand new flag pole to 44 year-old Thomas Theurkauf from Connecticut who was killed at the World Trade Center. Donated by Woodmen of the World and erected at the Oak Hill Middle School, the pole was surrounded by students, faculty, and staff as the flag was flown at half-mast.

Milledgeville received a $500,000 grant from the Employment Incentive Program (EIP) to improve the drainage problem we had been having behind the new Lowe's Home Improvement store. We applied for the grant in 2002 when we realized that Lowe's might be coming and that we could have a drainage problem on the proposed property. This was the first time in recent memory that we had received an EIP grant. It was a large sum of money, and I was glad that we would be able to improve the storm drainage.

On October 8, 2003, the city council named Councilman Ken Vance as its mayor pro-tem, a position that had been vacant for more than a year. When I first came into office, appointing a replacement was one of my duties, but under the new amended city charter, it fell to City Council. They appointed Vance by a vote of 5-0.

Also in October, the council hired Ron Rabun as interim city manager. However, before he could be named, council went into an executive session for 20 minutes to make budget amendments. Rabun was a resident of Griffin, Georgia, and had extensive experience in management. His first job as city manager had been in Camilla, Georgia. After that, he worked as county manager for Henry County, Georgia. He had also worked in several counties in Florida. Therefore, to someone who didn't know him well, Rabun seemed more than qualified for the job. Personally, however, I was not impressed. I perceived him to be a swindler and thought that the contract that Council had given him was outrageous. Furthermore, he was hard to monitor, at times coming in to work in the afternoons and, at other times, at 3 or 4 a.m.

My trip to Chicago in May, after being chosen as a HistoryMaker, showed exciting results in October. The Cleo Parker Robinson Dance Ensemble agreed to come to Milledgeville during the week of October 13th through the 19th. This amazing group of 13 dancers performs modern/jazz/ethnic dance routines drawn from a variety of dance traditions and strives to foster an appreciation for the art of dance in new audiences. Tying the visit to our bicentennial, Randy Cannon, director of Allied Arts, was beside himself with excitement. "It's just a community wide celebration of the bicentennial," he said. "This is one of the first African American dance companies that was founded in the U.S., over 30 years ago, so they have a long history as being one of the first."

The dance group performed at several middle and high schools and did a "balance and movement" workshop with the Baldwin County High School varsity basketball team that was very educational. They showed the players ways to avoid injury by centering and focusing movement. They also gave a free performance at the Russell Auditorium at Georgia College and State University on October 17th to a packed crowd. It was an amazing week and everyone who came in contact with these performers was affected in a positive way. They had such high levels of energy; it was impossible not to feel it.

Early in the month of December, we had a very memorable day. Every year since 1958, the Mayor's Christmas Motorcade, a parade sponsored by the Georgia Municipal Association, begins in

Milledgeville. Notables from around the state, including First Lady Mary Perdue, attended that year's event, which kicked off with a parade beginning in front of Central State Hospital. Marching bands from Georgia Military College and Washington County High School played throughout the parade, accompanied by floats ridden by CSH clients and personnel. After the parade, everyone assembled in the CSH auditorium for the Mayor's Day Program, where Marvin Bailey, CEO of Central State, welcomed everyone. Georgia's First Lady Mary Perdue spoke to the crowd, as did I and others. The auditorium was packed and was brilliantly decorated with Christmas ornaments from one end to the other. This program gave us an opportunity to welcome the Christmas season with the clients at Central State Hospital. It was a great way to kick off the holidays, and I hope the tradition continues.

Chapter 11

2004 in Office

The year 2004 started out well. On January 19th, the city held its annual MLK Day, complete with gospel music, a picnic, a march, and several speeches given in honor of Dr. Martin Luther King, Jr. Huley Park, the starting point of the day, was packed with more than 300 people as adults and children listened to gospel music. The SCLC (Southern Christian Leadership Conference) held its 12th annual celebration at Flagg Chapel Baptist Church, where Dr. Joshua Murfree, Jr., spoke on the 2004 theme *One Nation...One Dream—The Dream Is In Our Hands.* The church was packed with more than 200 people who listened attentively as Dr. Murfree challenged those present not to let King's dream of social justice die. "This is the kind of crowd that needs to be at the schools when something is wrong," he said. "You have to take a step out from where you are..... Have a vision, wake up." More than 100 people had marched from Huley Park to the new Black Heritage Memorial, then on to Flagg Chapel church. It was a great way to celebrate and honor King and his dream. I felt like the day was hugely successful.

In February, I filed suit against City Council—for the second time. This suit was similar to the one I had filed in September of 2003, and it stated that changing the city's charter to a city-manager form of government had stripped me of my power and discriminated against minority voters, who had elected me for a mayor-city council form of government but were being robbed of their expectation. I also charged that the city-charter change was designed to inflict punishment on me, personally.

Later that month, many residents of Milledgeville became fed up with the refusal of City Manager Ron Rabun and City Council to acknowledge their questions about the proposed budget, the change in the city charter and, to be frank, any other legitimate questions citizens had. Because of this, a group of concerned citizens, the Community Unity Organization (CUO), held a press conference early in March on the steps of City Hall and hand-delivered certified letters to City Council with questions they wanted answered. In one of the letters, Milledgeville citizen Annie Miller criticized the fact that City Council had not thoroughly researched Ron Rabun's background before hiring him. She questioned his termination from previous jobs and the fact that the city of Griffin, Rabun's previous employer, was in dire financial straits and had discovered an unauthorized $3 million withdrawal of funds from its city-owned power account. "We believe there are serious deficiencies in the research of recommendations and background in filling this important city position," Miller said. Rabun responded by hiring an attorney, Michael Caldwell from Atlanta, to demand that the group publicly retract its statements and stop talking about Rabun. City Councilman Ken Vance, supported by Dennette Jackson and Jeanette Walden, responded, "I do not respond to baseless interrogatories." (Translation: "I don't have to answer any questions that I don't want to.")

By the end of April, the Community Unity Organization was frustrated, but tireless. At a city-council meeting, several of the group's members were present and addressed their concerns to council members, hoping to get answers, since Rabun was rarely at meetings and was often out of town. When Donald Hill, a member of the CUO, asked the council why it had not responded to the group's letters and if council members had investigated Rabun's background before hiring him, Jeanette Walden said, "I did my homework before he was hired." When the same questions were put to Denise Shinholster, she replied that Rabun was an interim employee. When asked if Rabun had appointed any department heads, Shinholster replied, "I don't know how many times I have to say that Rabun is an interim city manager. As soon as we hire a permanent manager, we will uphold the charter." Citizen Beverly Calhoun then questioned the fact that much of the permanent decisions were being made by Milledgeville's "interim" city manager, and she questioned Council's plan to get started on hiring a permanent one. "You changed the charter that had been in place for more than 200 years," Calhoun said. "What was the purpose, if you weren't going to follow it?"

It was disheartening to watch the disdain that City Council held for the taxpayers that had voted them into office. Council's lack of interest was an indication of how elevated above the "common" citizen they considered themselves to be. Perhaps most indicative of their self-serving attitude was the remark Vance made when he was asked if he did his homework before voting to hire Rabun. "I've known Mr. Rabun since college," was all he said, as if friendship was the basis upon which to vote someone into such an important city office. I had a real problem with that.

After getting their way in changing the city charter, certain members of City Council seemed to feel that they were now the ones in power, and it showed in the complete disregard they displayed for rules of conduct during city-council meetings. There was often much crosstalk, arguing, and raised voices. It was like trying to talk to a bunch of school kids—simply no order, at times. Because of this, on April 22, I issued a memo stating that I had attempted to perform my duties at council meetings but had been unable to do so because of a lack of order at the meetings. Council members were disruptive, frequently interrupting me and talking among themselves, displaying an overall lack of respect for my position, as well as for their own positions as council members. Therefore, I announced that I was appointing a sergeant-at-arms to be present at all future council meetings to enforce compliance with the rules of conduct. This would allow meetings to be more productive.

Ron Rabun immediately struck down the idea, citing city code, which states that only he had the authority to make such an appointment and that if he decided to appoint someone, it would be a member of council. He stated that he felt it wasn't needed at that time. For someone who was rarely in attendance at city-council meetings, I failed to see how he could make that statement. I filed a suit against the council on May 18, and they were finally served with a summons the first week in July. Not long afterwards, I appeared on Fox 24's "Fox Files" program, a local 30-minute political show with a question-and-answer forum. Macon Mayor C. Jack Ellis had invited me on the show, and I saw this as an opportunity to answer questions about my daily struggles and frustrations with city council.

On August 24, city-council members voted unanimously to make Rabun the first permanent city manager of Milledgeville. Just three days after accepting the appointment, Rabun signed a contract to become the county administrator of Oconee County in South Carolina. Barry Jarrett, water and sewerage director, became the new interim city manager. City Council then scrambled around and offered the job to Mike Nettles, city manager of Altus, Oklahoma. Nettles accepted and signed the contract with the City of Milledgeville on September 14, 2004, but reneged on the contract less than a month later, opting to stay where he was rather than be subjected to close scrutiny by a group of concerned Milledgeville residents who had researched Nettles and discovered that he had been fired from manager jobs in St. Mary's and East Ridge, Tennessee. Mayor Pro-tem Vance was angry, stating that "a small group of people are trying to sabotage, criticize, and disrupt the processes of the City Council." I found Vance's complaint ridiculous, for if you put yourself in the position of a high-profile job, you should expect people to scrutinize your decisions. Evidently, Vance and other council members felt that they were exempt from that rule.

On October 12, City Council (namely, Mayor Pro-tem Councilman Vance) asked me to drop the two lawsuits I had pending against council. "What would really help us in our search (for a city manager) is for you to become....not necessarily an advocate, just quit being an adversary to the process," said Vance during a committee-of-the-whole meeting an hour before the regularly scheduled council meeting. "If you would drop these lawsuits that you aren't going to win and let this process proceed, then I think it would go a lot faster than it has up to this point," Vance told me. This request seemed to suggest that my legal attempt to reverse City Council's charter change had something to do with the council's failure to secure a city manager that would stay. I adamantly refused to comply. They wanted to strip me of my power, and they had succeeded—then they wanted me to accommodate their wishes? I wasn't going to do it. And the fact that council members were calling the aforementioned group of concerned citizens "headhunters" simply because they wanted to see a qualified person in office was ludicrous. As taxpayers and free citizens, they had the right to say anything they wanted to say, as well as the right to research any prospective city manager, since it appeared that City Council wasn't willing to do its homework.

At this point in time, members of the city council decided that they were going to start calling their own meetings. Fueling their belief that they could legally do this was city attorney Jimmy Morgan, who told them that nothing in the charter forbid them from doing so. My attorney and I informed them that the mayor always calls the meetings, regardless of the type of city charter—it says so in the charter. How they felt they were justified in interpreting the rules to justify their intention was ridiculous. The city charter also doesn't say that you can't hold meetings in the middle of a grocery store, but it doesn't take a rocket scientist to know that you don't do that.

Near the beginning of November, Ron Rabun released the recommended budget for the year 2004-2005. This was actually an 18-month budget that allowed an extra six-month period to bring our fiscal year into line. This "budget" increased the millage rate by 1 percent, an increase that equaled some $205,000. If council were to approve this budget, taxpayers would see a 10 percent increase in their utility bills, as well as an added $2.50 a month to keep the streets clean. It also included a 2 percent wage increase for all city employees not under contract. Doug Hawkins, city finance director with whom Rabun had composed the budget, spelled it out succinctly. "We quickly made the assumption that there was no way to make the budget balance…with the added expenses in the budget," he said. "One would have to conclude that the funds had to come from somewhere." These "added expenses" amounted to Rabun's paycheck—$130,500, over the course of the 18 months. When office costs and other benefits were added in, it came to a whopping more than $238,000 to fund Rabun's position. I was completely against this; I felt it was a slap in the face to the citizens of Milledgeville who had voted for a mayor, not a city manager. Seventy-five percent of this tax increase would be going to pay his salary.

Frankly, I was relieved when Rabun reneged for a better job and left the council in a lurch. Had he stayed, I think Milledgeville would have suffered financially in more ways than one.

Griffin vs. City Council

On November 30, 2004, my state lawsuit against the Milledgeville City Council for changing the form of government went to trial at the Baldwin County Superior Court. At issue were two things: whether or not the change in the form of government in the middle of a mayor's term was constitutional, and who has the power to appoint a sergeant-at-arms at council meetings. Superior Court Judge William Towson didn't issue a ruling, but instead gave both sides ten days to submit their orders to his court.

On December 15, Judge Towson ruled in the city council's favor, stating in his order: "The court finds that there is no dispute of a genuine issue of material fact, that the challenged legislation was not constitutionally flawed, and that the office of the Mayor has not been abolished." Towson also ruled against me on the sergeant-at-arms issue, stating that City Council could appoint such a person if they felt the need. I believed that Judge Towson had ruled incorrectly, and I had my attorney immediately file an appeal with the Georgia Supreme Court. I also planned to continue my federal lawsuit and was then awaiting a court date in the U.S. District Court in Macon, Georgia.

Also by December 15, the city council closed the application process for a new city manager. They would be choosing from the resumes sent to them up to that point, they said—a total of 19 applicants. The job of each council member, after being given a copy of each applicant's package, was to whittle down that number to five choices. During the first week of January 2005, they were to come together in agreement and decide on the top three candidates. They would then interview each one and choose whom they thought was best qualified for the job.

I found it interesting that suddenly Councilman Vance changed his point of view. For months he had argued that my lawsuits against City Council were interfering with council members' ability to hire and keep a city manager—"scaring off potential candidates," I believe were his words. Now he was singing a different tune, saying that the candidates were not, after all, frightened off by my lawsuits. "They know our situation and they're comfortable with it," Vance said. "They know about the mayor suing the city council and the lawsuits and so forth. They also know about the previous city-manager candidates." This was a big switch, but such vacillation wasn't an unusual thing for Vance and other council members.

Saving Children and Laying Indignity to Rest

Fortunately, my 2004 year in office was not solely defined by the struggles I endured with my city colleagues. There were also rewards, as well as obstacles that were rewarding to overcome. On August 28, the summer meeting of the Georgia Conference of Black Mayors (GCBM) met at Fort Valley State College. Mayors from Atlanta to Vidalia came to represent their cities. Also present was then-State Representative Tyrone Brooks, representing GABEO (Georgia Association of Black Elected Officials). Conference attendees decided to lend our support to the National Prostate Cancer Awareness Month Campaign and to work on a plan to aid the Center for Missing and Exploited Children. Michelle Kourouma, executive director of the National Conference of Black Mayors (NCBM), brought information on new programs and grants being offered by the NCBM. As always, it was an informative and inspiring meeting, and I left with new, fresh ideas and confirmation that I was on the right track.

On September 9, Internal Affairs members of city council requested an audit to access where the city stood in our budget. I had written a memo requesting this audit on the 2nd of September because we were nine months into our 18-month fiscal year and had yet to receive a monthly report on accounts payable and receivable. In fact, Councilwoman Denise Shinholster had been asking for reports for months. Julia Lake, the interim finance director, cited the switch to a new computer system as the reason for not generating reports for such a long period of time.

Toward the end of September, at a council meeting, I was pleased to announce that Affordable Equity, Inc., had been approved to build a 54-unit housing development for the elderly at the corner of Montgomery and Pickens streets. This unit would be named Pecan Hills. I had pushed for this for the past couple of years, and the Department of Community Affairs (DCA) finally approved a partnership between the City of Milledgeville and Affordable Equity

Partners, Inc. DCA Commissioner Mike Beatty was very supportive of the idea from the beginning. He had visited the proposed site the year before, and I had talked with him by phone numerous times, in my efforts to make it happen. Finally, through the collaboration of various organizations, the development became a reality.

The month of October brought more social advancement in Milledgeville. When the Rivers Building at Central State Hospital was constructed in 1938-1939, the remains of some 2,000 African Americans were moved from what residents called the "old colored cemetery" to three mass graves. Nearly sixty years later, an effort began to correct this past injustice. The Cemetery Memorial Project began in 1997 as a way to restore Cedar Lane Cemetery at Central State Hospital and bring dignity and respect to the remains of past clients of the hospital. In October of 2004, Milledgeville held a ceremony to dedicate two beautiful headstones in honor of those whose remains had been relocated. Central State Hospital CEO Marvin Bailey had been working on behalf of the cemetery for years, and I was glad we were finally able to achieve the goal. During the ceremony, Bailey reminded onlookers that the site had been listed on the Georgia Historic Register in May and that he was working on having it listed on the National Historic Register.

The following month, I announced with a mixture of excitement and humility that Milledgeville would be one of only five cities in the state to take part in the new program for missing and exploited children that was coming in January. This was a program that the Georgia Conference of Black Mayors had wholeheartedly decided to support in past GCBM meetings. The National Conference of Black Mayors had chosen Georgia as the state to receive this honor, and since I was president of the Georgia conference, I had the responsibility of choosing the five cities that would receive the pilot program. Of course, I chose Milledgeville as one of the five. This was an awesome new program that didn't cost the city a dime, and what we received could not be measured in dollar amounts. The program provided us with a $5,000 Canon camera screener and printer with which we could produce identification CDs of children. The data would be stored in a national database, and should a child disappear, the CDs would help law enforcement locate the missing child. I was honored that Milledgeville would be one of the first to institute this new and much-needed law-enforcement aid.

By December, work on our Streetscape Project was in full force. I knew that the one-way flow of traffic from the corner of Hancock and Jefferson streets was inconvenient, and I was pleased that construction of the sidewalks along that area was progressing smoothly. Despite all the troubles throughout the year with city council, Milledgeville continued to blossom and grow, consistent with my vision for progress for our city. I knew in my heart that 2005 held many nice things for Milledgeville, and I was determined to see them through.

Chapter 12

2005: Lawsuits and Other Differences

One of the first encouraging experiences of the new year of 2005 occurred on January 13, when local officials and representatives of several non-profit organizations met to discuss the possibility of much-needed affordable housing in Milledgeville. We had, as many cities do, a segment of city residents who were living in less-than-desirable conditions, and we wanted to see what could be done about it. We called this meeting because Millard Fuller, who founded Habitat for Humanity, and his wife Linda, had visited Milledgeville the year before and noticed a large amount of substandard homes. I promised Fuller, at the time of his visit, that I would do something about it.

The January meeting was open-forum in nature and several groups were represented, including the Middle Georgia Regional Development Center, Habitat for Humanity, Rivers Alive, Overview, Inc., and the local housing authority. We called this initiative the Milledgeville Affordable Housing Strategic Plan. Our goal: to secure a grant from CHIP (Community Home Investment Program). To do this, we needed to assess the various pockets of substandard housing throughout the city and develop a plan to upgrade them.

Harold Tessendorf, executive director of the Milledgeville /Baldwin County Habitat for Humanity, was present at the meeting and felt that involvement of different agencies was a good idea. "Habitat itself has a strategic goal of making substandard housing morally basically unacceptable," he said, "so I think this initiative, this collaborative that's coming together involving the city, involving non-profits, involving the housing authority, is very positive."

During the first week in February, the collaborative efforts of the Georgia Conference of Black Mayors and the National Center for Missing and Exploited Children produced tangible results. This effort to keep our children safer became a reality as we kicked-off the program, named Hand in Hand with Children, at Eagle Ridge Elementary School. The purpose of the program was introduce to adults and children alike, programs that educate them on techniques and tools that help keep all of our children safer. The following week, students in local elementary schools would be photographed and fingerprinted and this information would be transferred to a StreetSentz card that each parent would keep. In the event that a child disappeared or became lost, the parent would take the ID card to the police station where officials would make up flyers, contact NCMEC, and forward the child's information to Levi's Call, Georgia's version of the Amber Alert.

After a week of programs within the local schools educating children about ways to stay safe, Saturday was the big day. Beginning at 10am at the Milledgeville Mall, local police officials were on hand to photograph and fingerprint kids for their ID cards. I was surprised and pleased to see that literally hundreds of people showed up with their kids to take advantage of the program. The turnout was phenomenal; this week had turned out to be a huge success from day one. This was just another of my dreams of forward movement for Milledgeville realized.

February also saw another great Arbor Day celebration. I proclaimed February 15th as Georgia Arbor Day and we solidified this proclamation by planting several trees in Huley Park. We planted an

8-foot October Glory that the Old Capitol Garden Club had donated, as well as two dogwoods and a crepe myrtle, donated by the Georgia Forestry Commission. The following day, Saturday, we continued to celebrate Arbor Day at the Georgia Veterans Memorial Cemetery, where more trees were planted and the Georgia Military College Band performed. State Representative Kenneth Birdsong, Fred Allen (director of the Georgia Forestry Commission), Pete Wheeler (Department of Veterans Affairs Commissioner), and many others attended the event. City maintenance crews dug the holes for the plantings and provided the mulch for the new trees.

During our winter GCBM meeting for 2005, we mayors went on record opposing the proposed voter photo ID legislation. This was a piece of legislation that if passed, would require voters to produce a state-issued picture ID in order to vote. We felt that this law would seriously disenfranchise a number of our society's groups, including the poor, the minorities, and the elderly. There were a number of individuals present at this meeting that were vehemently opposed to the legislation, including president of GABEO (Georgia Association of Black Elected Officials) Tyrone Brooks, Lt Governor Mark Taylor, Labor Commissioner Michael Thurmond, and Georgia state Senator Robert Brown. Said Brown, "It's clear what's going on here. Republicans want to maximize their opportunities and minimize ours. We want to be sure the world hears our cry of opposition to this."

Lawsuit Stalled

Not so positive, however, were the battles I continued to have with the city council. In fact, in this arena, the year 2005 began much as 2004 had ended—with resistance to nearly every decision I made. On top of that, on January 20, I was greatly disappointed when the Georgia Supreme Court docketed my case against the council and decided not to hear it until April. I had hoped to have some kind of finality to this early in the year, but that was not to be. However,

I received bad news earlier than I expected. In a summary judgment on February 28, U.S. District Court Judge Duross Fitzpatrick struck down my federal lawsuit against Governor Sonny Perdue, former Senator Faye Smith, Representative Bobby Parham, and the six members of the Milledgeville City Council. I believe that when the Justice Department pre-cleared the legislation for the change in the city charter, my lawsuit became an uphill battle from then on.

I decided to appeal Judge Fitzpatrick's decision, and I had help from a few powerful friends. Near the beginning of March, the Rainbow/PUSH Coalition (RPC) filed an *amicus curiae* (friend of the court) petition with the Georgia Supreme Court, on my behalf. Amicus *curiae* is a legal brief prepared by a person or group who is not involved in a court case but has an interest in its outcome. Rainbow/PUSH was founded by the Rev. Jesse Jackson and is a merger of Operation PUSH, formed in 1971, and the Rainbow Coalition, founded in 1985. RPC's organizational literature states that the group is dedicated to "improving the lives of all people by focusing on cures for social, economic, and political ills." From the beginning of my court battles, RPC Southeast Regional Director Joe Beasley had followed my efforts to reverse the city-charter change. "I was disappointed, quite frankly, when City Council undertook to strip his real power from him," Beasley said about me. "RPC very much encouraged Mr. Griffin to seek some legal redress. We want to know the rationale of why the city council wanted to strip him of his power when it's clear that he's done a good job." Beasley offered his own answer: "It's pretty clear, at least from my reading into it, that there are some race issues involved in the matter," he said, and he added: "I don't understand how the African American city-council members would be a part of that. Black people have been so conditioned to being under white leadership that sometimes black people are their own worst enemies. I think that's what's going on over there with the black city-council people.....Many of us still want to be on the plantation." Others who decided to submit similar briefs on my behalf included the Georgia Conference of Black Mayors, the Community Unity Committee of Milledgeville, and Mayor C. Jack Ellis of Macon.

On March 1, 2005, City Council finally managed to hire a city manager. E. Scott Wood was chosen and signed the contract to become the first permanent city manager for Milledgeville under the new charter. Now members of City Council were arguing among themselves about Wood's contract. It seems that the contract he signed promised him an annual salary of $95,000 when the budget and the advertisement for a city manager listed a salary closer to $87,000. I had to agree with Denise Shinholster and Richard Mullins that this was an illegal act, despite the other council members' excuses for the change. Personally, I was also disturbed by the fact that the contract never stated how much it was going to cost the city of Milledgeville to hire and sustain Wood's position across the board. The whole thing was mishandled, but I suppose council was in a hurry to get someone into position because of their failures to do so in the past.

In April, my federal lawsuit against the Milledgeville City Council was dismissed because of a lack of action on my part. I wasn't hurt by the decision, though, because I had decided, after all, not to pursue my case at the federal level. Instead, I wanted to concentrate my efforts in the Georgia Supreme Court, so I let the deadline to file paperwork in federal court pass by.

Interview with Tyrone Brooks,
Georgia State Representative and President of GABEO
(Georgia Association of Black Elected Officials):

"Floyd was a mayor before his time. His vision for Milledgeville was a vision that was not acceptable and not understood by many people, especially elected officials, because some of the things he was advocating many people just weren't ready for. He wanted to make Milledgeville a first-class city; he wanted to put Milledgeville on the map as being not only one of the first capitals of Georgia, but also being more than

just the home of Central State Hospital. Floyd had a very aggressive agenda and he tried to get City Council and others to buy into his agenda."

"Floyd was trying to move Milledgeville in a different way and some weren't ready for that. It's not unusual for there to be disagreement. But it is unusual for elected officials to turn on such a person as Floyd in a very serious, very unprofessional way. I saw some of the attacks coming that were very personal, so I tried to get Floyd to focus on the big picture, to move on to something else."

"Being mayor, Floyd had to learn to accommodate other opinions, to accept other ideas, to compromise. Sometimes, the art of compromise will be the catalyst to your success as a public official. The great elected officials of our time have been those who have been able to accommodate the ideals and positions and, sometimes, the agendas of others, and incorporate them into the big picture."

"So he did have a rocky road with this council; he did have some differences with members of the council that became very personal. It got into the media, and that was disappointing. Just looking at all of the major cities where you have strong mayors and a strong mayor form of government, you always have the clashes between the mayor and the council. Maynard Jackson and Andrew Young had that problem; it's not unusual. And Floyd being the first black mayor of Milledgeville, he was a target for some people who did not want to see a black person as the mayor of Milledgeville. There were a lot of people who didn't give him a chance."

"Milledgeville's population in the inner city is majority white. The senatorial district that he won was majority white, so when he ran, I believed that the kind of race he was going to run would be appealing across the spectrum. And sure enough, he won. But he became a target immediately for those who had been against him—the antagonists and some people in the local media. Some people didn't want a black person who was strong-willed and outspoken and wouldn't be a yes person or someone who would go along to get along—[but was] highly opinionated. I knew he was going to be a target, so Dr. [Joseph] Lowery and I counseled him. We said, "Look, Floyd. We're going to be with you, but it's not going to be easy." Dr. Lowery, being the sage of the Movement that he is, he could talk to Floyd in a way that resonated with some of the things he was going to have to contend with."

"Floyd becoming the first black mayor of Milledgeville was similar to a woman breaking through the corporate glass ceiling. There will always be people on the other side just waiting to criticize you, just waiting to make it difficult for you to succeed. They would do things to a woman that they would never dream of doing to a man. It was the same way with Floyd."

"Floyd's road became rough because he decided he was going to be different. He decided he was going to step out of the box. He recognized that there would be persons who would oppose him, but he said, 'This is the right thing to do. I have to do it.'"

"The criticism of Floyd's ideas and vision wasn't substantive criticism, it was personal criticism. Criticism around substance and real ideas is okay, but criticism simply because of a personality, I think, is very divisive and unethical. If I'm just going to criticize you because of who you are and not based on the issues, I think I'm being a hypocrite. And I saw a great deal of hypocrisy from those critics who were leveling accusations and all kinds of charges and just voting against his agenda because they could. I've seen that in other levels of the body politic, as well. In Atlanta, Shirley Franklin's had the same problem because she's a woman, the first black female mayor. Were it not for the Atlanta Journal & Constitution being supportive and friendly to her agenda, Shirley would not have survived."

"Floyd is a man of ideas. I like people with ideas. You may not always agree with them, but you can usually find some ideas that this person has articulated to agree with, and I enjoy that. I've watched Floyd and he's always thinking of something new, trying to do something different, some new proposal to write. He's innovative and creative."

On May 12th, Milledgeville hosted a regional career expo at Georgia College and State University to promote job growth in the area. This came about after a conversation I had in 2004 with Georgia Department of Labor Commissioner Michael Thurmond about how to instigate job growth in Middle Georgia. We came up with the idea of a job fair and it was a very good idea. Approximately 60-70 businesses showed up at the fair, a lot of them Baldwin County businesses. This was a successful event, with many unemployed and employed individuals attending to see what was out there.

By the summer of 2005, the pilot program that I had helped institute in five cities in Georgia for the NCMEC (National Center for Missing and Exploited Children) had gained national recognition and would be used as a national model for other states. I was invited to Washington DC to present our model of "Hand in Hand With Children: Guiding and Protecting" during a two-day conference that was designed to unite and mobilize communities all over the country to help protect our children. The conference was a very humbling, yet rewarding, experience for me. Savannah mayor Otis Johnson and were called on to discuss the program and how it works, which was followed by a question and answer period. I was honored to be able to speak one-on-one with Ralph Basham, Director of the Secret Service, and Rebecca Turner Gonzales, the attorney general's wife. Both were interested in Milledgeville's history and I extended them an invitation to visit at any time. This was a very good opportunity to give Milledgeville and the state of Georgia some very good exposure about what we are and what we are doing here for our children.

In June, the City of Milledgeville received a grant of over $12,000 from the Department of Community Affairs to fund a local housing assessment. Although the housing conditions in the city had not been one of my platform issues when running for the office of mayor, it had since become a major focus for me. Last year, I had set up a housing task force that included me, the zoning director, the fire chief, the housing authority, Habitat for Humanity, Overview and the River of Life. The primary goals of this collaboration were to secure grants that would help provide affordable housing for all of our citizens.

Because of this group, the city was awarded a Community Development Block Grant in 2004 to make drainage improvements in a specific area so that Habitat for Humanity could come in and build homes. This most recent grant was for an assessment that would provide a complete picture of the city's housing situation, therefore showing us what grants we needed and how and where to utilize them.

In August, many factions of the public were very interested in what my political plans were for the end of this year. I had been thinking about my options for the past several months, which included, but were not limited to, a run for U.S. Congress, a bid for re-election as Milledgeville's mayor, or a run for the District 25 Senate seat, which I had already held once before. I decided to announce my intentions on the Quintin T. Howell radio talk show because I had been the on his show several times in the past and I felt this was a good way to let the public know where I stood. On August 29th, I held a press conference and announced that I would seek re-election as Milledgeville's mayor for a second term. I had made a commitment to the citizens who believed in me enough to elect me the first time around and there were still things that I would like to see done, new heights that Milledgeville could rise to. After careful consideration and discussions with my family and members of the community, I decided to try to come back for another four years.

It was also in August that U.S. Representative John Barrow appointed me to his military academy advisory committee. The committee is a group of people who screen applicants for the nation's military academies, based on each applicant's character and his commitment to his academic success and to his community and his country. We then make recommendations to U.S. Representative Barrow, who is allowed to nominate 10 individuals for each of the country's four military academies. "I am excited that Mayor Griffin has agreed to join this important committee," U.S. Representative Barrow said. "As a retired Colonel in the U.S. Army and as a longtime leader here in Milledgeville, Mayor Griffin knows just what it takes to succeed in one's service to both country and community. And those are just the qualities we are looking for in our nominees." I was very flattered by U.S. Representative Barrow's faith and trust in my abilities to recognize the necessary qualities in applicants for the academies.

On September 13th, we held the groundbreaking for the Pecan Hills elderly living complex. Project Manager Carrie Jarrett was on hand to explain the partnering between Affordable Equity Partners, Inc, who had issued the grant to build, and local service agencies to assist the mostly elderly individuals who would be living in the complex. "We have an understanding with Oconee Regional Medical Center to provide many of the health services such as testing and lab work," Jarrett said. "We also have a contract with the mental health arena. We developed this health care model because most of the tenants will be elderly and will need to stay connected with their community doctors and services." City council voted to abate the property taxes for the first five years; 100% the first year; 80% the second and third year; 40% the fourth year; and 20% the final year. After two years in the planning, we would finally see this vision come to fruition. The summer of 2006 was tentatively slated for completion of the project.

September is National Prostate Cancer Awareness month and on September 14th, we held the annual free prostate cancer screening at Oconee Urology, PC. This is a yearly event to help the public become more aware that 1 in 6 men in the country will develop prostate cancer. The 100 Black Men of Milledgeville is also very involved in this campaign. Several local urologists were present, including Drs. Fred Stewart and Boris Velimironovich. Dr. Velimironovich commented on the success of the program. "Since we got involved with the mayor's office and 100 Men, the number of screened men increased about 50%, so it's becoming more like a big health fair," he said.

It was about this time that I attended the 31st annual National Conference of Black Mayors in Columbus, Ohio. This was a great 4-day conference, attended by more than 2,000 people and over 300 black mayors. It was there that I was awarded a $6,000 cash incentive for my work on the Challenge to Buckle Up America initiative between NCBM and the National Highway Traffic Safety Administration. When I had attended the NCBM annual conference the past couple of years, I had noticed other mayors taking on this initiative and I wanted to do this with Milledgeville, so when I returned last year, I talked to Police Chief Woodrow Blue and discussed it with him. At that point, we started a 3-phase program of awareness, education, and enforcement. "We just tried to make everybody aware of the problems with not buckling up that we have in the community," Chief Blue said. "During the educational phase, we tried to educate the kids on why it's important to buckle up. We had several workshops," he said. "The third phase was the enforcement side, where we went out and enforced the seat belt law. I'm very proud of the work and the results that the effort had on making seat belt use more prevalent in our community — it saves lives," he concluded. When I received the check, I gave it to the Milledgeville Police Department.

Qualifying began in September for upcoming elections. All six seats of the city council were up for election and I wouldn't have minded seeing all six council members replaced. They had been, largely, a "do nothing" council for the entire 4 years and while they complained loudly about me not wanting to work with anyone and succeeded in taking away most of my power, I had still accomplished most of what I had set out to do in the beginning, and then some. They, on the other hand, had accomplished nothing more than a change in the form of government in an attempt to keep me from doing anything. Richard Bentley qualified for the mayoral election, so it looked to be a mayor's race much like the one 4 years before.

In October, Richard Bentley asserted that his campaign had been attacked by phone calls over a 3 week period to registered voters. The phone call was a recorded message by a female accusing Bentley of receiving campaign contributions from special interests groups that would benefit if he were to be elected mayor. Because there were only the two of us in the mayor's race, Bentley jumped to the conclusion that I had something to do with it, or at the very least, I should find out who it was and punish them. I had no idea who taped that message, nor did I care. If your campaign funds are legitimate, then you have nothing to worry about. I couldn't find the energy to get upset about it. And the idea that it was my job as mayor to find out who did it and punish them was ludicrous. How was I supposed to do that? I felt like it was just a lot of unnecessary publicity over nothing.

But I did want monitoring of the voting process, especially in the area of absentee voting, so I requested that the Secretary of State's office send someone down to Milledgeville to make sure all aspects of the elections were fair and legal. I had been hearing some things from the public that there were individuals trying to pressure people into voting by absentee ballot. This was possible because House Bill 244 had passed recently, allowing people to vote absentee without having a valid reason, such as being out of town on election day. Therefore, more and more people were calling and requesting absentee ballots, probably for convenience. House Bill 244 also suspended the requirement of a photo ID when voting absentee, making it much easier for those without identification to vote through an absentee ballot. The office of the Secretary of State agreed to send officials to monitor the voting process, after which their recorded statements about what they observed would be reviewed by the state in order to ensure legitimacy of the process.

In an effort to "get back" at me for the recorded phone message about him that I had nothing to do with, Richard Bentley decided to send out a flyer about me stating "Floyd Griffin has sued you. Not once, but twice! Floyd Griffin has sued the citizens and the City of Milledgeville twice...... We have to pay our tax money to defend ourselves from Floyd's lawsuits." This was an absurd attack. I sued City Council for changing the form of government after I was elected and they chose to use taxpayer money for their defense fund. The money behind my state and federal lawsuits came out of my own pocket. The flyer was just ridiculous. Never in my entire political career had I witnessed a candidate stoop so low in order to win an election. It was pretty indicative of just how immature and childish Richard Bentley really was. I lost the election. The next morning, I called Bentley to congratulate him and offered my cooperation as a professional courteousy. I reminded him that I was doing what he had not done when I won the runoff election against him in 2001.

On Saturday, November 19th, the 100 Black Men of America Milledgeville Oconee Chapter met in the Goldstein Center for Performing Arts at the Georgia Military College to present several awards to various community members. Dr. Janet Hogan-Harrison, Dr. Martha Williams, Jeanie Jarrett, Johnnie S. Wilson, Louise Austin, and the Milledgeville Mall all received top honors, with Austin receiving the Mentor Award, 100 Black Men's highest honor, for her work with Milledgeville youth. I was presented a trailblazer award and I, in turn, presented trailblazer awards to Bobby Knox and Herman Rozier for their contribution to making a path of change in the community. This event was the first of what would be an annual program to honor those who tirelessly give to their communities.

In December, I was named to the board of directors of the National Center for Missing and Exploited Children. I was extremely honored to receive this appointment as only a handful of people from the southeast United States were chosen to serve. "Floyd is a highly skilled, highly respected public servant who brings an array of expertise and unwavering commitment to the National Center," said NCMEC President and CEO Ernie Allen. "He has an extensive record of success and I am confident that his election to our Board will be invaluable." The "Hand in Hand With Children: Guiding and Protecting" campaign had meant a lot to me from its very inception; that's why I had put so much time and effort into getting it implemented all over the United States.

Mayor Griffin briefing Civil Rights Legend Rev. Joseph L. Lowery.

Senator Griffin with Georgia State Representative Billy McKinney.

Chapter 13

My Conclusions:
Concerns About the Black Community

I am worried that the black community has become too comfortable. Many of us have luxury cars, ranch-style and two-story homes, and careers that pay good money. Consequently, the pangs of poverty don't hound the majority of our neighbors, as it once did, and those of us who have material comforts begin to worry more about keeping our acquisitions and less about helping those who don't have much. As a result, we are no longer involved in our communities as activists. We don't volunteer in large numbers, and our men don't go to church as often as our women. Too many of us are playing golf, watching sports games, and sleeping, instead of making time for God and mentoring our youth. Therefore, far too many of the coming generation have chosen life in the fast lane over a more purpose-driven life that causes one to appreciate the sacrifices our fore parents made. To support this style of living, some will do anything, even stealing their neighbor's possessions, robbing innocent merchants, selling pleasure-producing poison—even to children—and murdering anyone who gets in their way. This makes my last concern an obvious one: Black folks don't seem to like each other as much as we once did.

If we continue along this dreary path, we'll have greater problems in the future. My hope is that we can recover from some of our community ills by refocusing on the issues that face us and reinforcing the importance of getting an education, being prepared for the practical aspects of adulthood, and showing respect to others. This should be even more true for the black community. Since politics plays an integral role in structuring the strategic moves that blacks need to make, we need to reconsider the type of leadership we select or allow to affect us. I think we should embrace a modern and inclusive-thinking leadership that can address the pertinent issues of today. This doesn't mean, however, that we should stop appreciating our civil-rights leaders. Never that! The quality of life we now enjoy was made possible by people like the Rev. Joseph E. Lowery. He and others of his generation laid the foundation for us to groom new leadership at the next levels. They provided for me the confidence to position myself to consider political leadership in local and state government.

But we still have a long way to go.

Black Leadership versus White Resistance

Black leadership versus white resistance in a town like Milledgeville, Georgia, in a place where there has been continual white control for a very long time, can become a contentious and even dangerous matter, especially when the one holding leadership is a black male. And when he seeks a position of absolute leadership—control over not just people but *money*—white resistance is even greater because money is the resource that rules the world. Whites, especially white men, have traditionally found it difficult to accept a black man having that much control and responsibility.

Many of the first black mayors of cities in this country faced greater challenges and problems than any of their predecessors faced. The trailblazing black mayor's success in office was often clouded by resistance from those under his charge or in his administration who had problems submitting to a black man's leadership. Examples of this can be seen in the stories of the mayoral careers of great men such as Harold Washington of Chicago, Carl Stokes in Cleveland, Maynard Jackson of Atlanta, and Richard Hatcher of Gary, Indiana. Vehement resistance is sometimes displayed by people who serve in small cities and towns. I know: Eight months after I was sworn in as the first black mayor of the 199-year-old Milledgeville, members of the city council, acting with the approval of some in the community, voted to change the city government from a strong-mayor structure to one that installed a city manager as a means of weakening the power of the mayoral office.

I am convinced that a major reason the whites of the City Council wanted the charter change is because the existing one gave the mayor—me, specifically—a particular authority that they openly and in unison resisted. In the event that the six members of the council were deadlocked in a tie vote, the traditional city charter dictated that only the mayor could break the tie. At the beginning of my administration, that gave me the controlling vote. Of course, whites on the council didn't like that; they knew who would be controlling the direction of the city if the three blacks voted together on most issues. Sadly, the harmony that the whites feared did not become a reality. The three white council members were often able to persuade the three black members to fall into the same resistant struggle against me. It saddened me that these blacks couldn't see the big picture, which was an opportunity to place in the hands of a black man absolute control over a city where whites had exclusively possessed such control for nearly 200 years.

So deluded were the three black council members that they played a major role in supporting the city-charter change that stripped away much of my mayoral authority and their power. But their actions came full circle, for under the new city-manager arrangement, occasions arose in which the council was split along racial lines. The new city charter dictated that the mayor would cast the tie-breaking vote. The three black council members who had refused to take a position of voting in harmony with me saw their white counterparts do so, siding with the mayor, who was white. In other words, they understood too late that, in the end, whites will do what any self-preserving group does that has power: band together (or, in this case, *vote* together) to ensure the members *keep* that power.

I ran for mayor with a platform and a vision, which is something the city needed. Neither of my opponents offered a real platform. The opponents were two white men who were probably ushered into the election because of their connections, not because they offered strong visions for change. The incumbent had been in politics for a number of years and hadn't done well in his administration; the other candidate was a businessman with no previous political experience. I had an excellent military background and proven political experience. Still, the race had to go into a runoff before I could claim a victory.

The first time I ran for mayor, I ended up in a runoff with an individual who had no political experience. I needed 78 votes to win without a runoff and I ended up winning by 21 votes in the runoff; the voting pretty much followed along racial lines. The voting pattern indicated I was going to have difficulty leading the city, and I did have continuous resistance. The election also highlighted a double standard, for if my opponent had possessed my background and experience and I, his experience, there would not have been a contest or runoff at all. This shows that the standards have to be much higher for blacks when they run for office and while they are serving in office. Those of my generation have always known this. Sadly, many blacks today act as if they have forgotten that. Quite often, these blacks make excuses for being black, and they monitor how they respond and act, instead of being what they are.

While I was in the Army, I rose to the rank of full colonel. I had a few very close friends that made general, which is a higher rank. I couldn't very well tell them how to be a general when I had never been one! Similarly, when I was battalion commander, none of my junior officers ever tried to tell me how to run my battalion. Yet, that is the experience I had when I served as mayor of Milledgeville. I had more black people than you can shake a stick at trying to tell me how to carry out my role as mayor. Instead of being patient and compassionate, they became overly critical and tried to make everything a public issue. There are ways to deal with concerns in a decent manner, but if people don't understand the political process, they often don't handle their concerns in a productive way and therefore become more of a problem than part of the solution. Blacks like the ones that resisted me fail to realize that if we have never before had a black person in a particular seat or office, we need to give the individual the opportunity to be successful, which means blacks should not become overly critical of the person blazing the trail. The new individual is going to make mistakes—how can he *not,* if this is a position he has never held before. We as a people have to remember that there were no black political and elected officials until just a few decades ago. The Civil Rights legislation was passed in 1965. So when we get a pioneering black in a political position, we should be supportive as he puts forth a diligent effort to learn the ropes. Only in this way can black leaders get what their white counterparts have had for generations, namely, the chance to grow, flourish, correct past mistakes, and achieve the power needed to make success happen. I pray that we will give President Barack Obama the opportunity to grow and flourish so that he will become the best President ever.

Reflections From Nathalie

Floyd and I have traveled over the past four decades along a road which has led us from college, into the military, into politics and business. It has not always been an easy journey, but together we became a family; together we raised two successful sons, together we have strengthened our Christian faith; together we have enjoyed the love and support of family and friends.

Floyd is my very best friend. We can sit in a room together and not say a word, but each knows what the other is thinking. We have both been blessed and we are indeed thankful each day. I look forward to growing older together.

America Makes History

In 2008, there is only one African American in the U.S. Senate. Not until this year did the majority of Americans, of all races, believe that a black man could actually become President. I didn't think that I would see this day during my lifetime.

When Senator Barack Obama announced his candidacy two years ago, I supported him then and I felt deep down that he had a good chance of winning.

I met Democratic Candidate for President Senator Obama in February of 2008, at his hotel before he spoke at Harvest Cathedral Church in Macon, Georgia. We talked about my being the first black elected in a majority white senatorial district and mayor in a predominately white southern city he said "Then you know what I'm up against." I certainly did.

I literally got chill bumps during the 11:00 P.M. hour when I and the world learned that he was our new president-elect. I feel that he will do great things for this nation. I wish my father had lived another three years to see this day.

It would be a good thing, for at any level of government, blacks in office usually attempt to make life better not just for blacks, but for the community at large. Together, we've got to make it happen.

President Obama is the finest example of a legacy to a legend. He is in fact, one of many who embrace the notion of academic preparedness, and a mindset that asks "what can

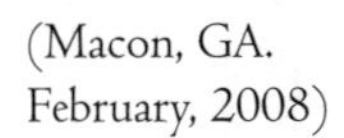
(Macon, GA.
February, 2008)

I do to create a positive change and make a difference. Each new generation is the beneficiary of the sacrifices, hopes and dreams of their fore parents. Inspired by the courage and Christian resolve of many who have served as leaders for a cause be it equal rights, freedom of expression, social or education reform, or fair wages, the many have seen themselves as the legacy who became a legend who inspires us all. They are responsible for making the world or community a better place through their efforts. I have been grateful to serve in the military during tumultuous times and have served my community, state and nation as a public official and administrator. These opportunities placed me in positions to make history in a couple of instances. I have served honorably in the spirit of many who came before me. They include my parents, Booker T. Washington, Dr. Martin Luther King, Jr., Mrs. Rosa Parks, Fannie Lou Hamer, Joe Louis, Jackie Robinson, Dr. Charles Drew, Dr. Ben Carson, General Colin Powell and of course, President Barack Obama, and many, many others. We all inspire one another. It is my fervent hope that my story will be an inspiration to our youth and others who can get excited about educational achievement, leadership and giving back to their community, state, and nation. The foundation of a good education, an unselfish mind and spirit of principle will put them on a path to success. This is the true direction of a *winner that makes it happen.*

Floyd L. Griffin Jr. Headlines - An Abridged Summary

Compiled by Janet Walker
(Taken from senator's scrapbook of newspaper clippings.)

PART I: 1994-1996—BUSINESSMAN AND SENATOR

SENATORIAL RUN

Retired colonel to seek Senate seat

Jan. 20, 1994, The Jones County News (perhaps Gray, GA) (Kathy Jefcoats, reporter)

Griffin's Friday announcement of intent to run for 25th District Senate seat then held by one-term incumbent Wilbur Baugh. Quotes Griffin's criticism of Baugh, including the incumbent's lack of communication with voters and contentious relationships with other state leaders.

Griffin attacks record of incumbent Baugh

April 26, 1994, The Union-Recorder, Milledgeville, GA (Johnathan Burns, reporter)

The day after paying the $400 qualifying fee to run for the 25th District seat, Griffin tells an audience of some 50 (at the Baldwin County High School Auditorium) that Baugh has repeatedly forsaken his constituents' best interests and has been inaccessible during his first term in the Senate—in effect, has been an empty seat. Griffin claims his platform rests on: 1) crime, 2) education, 3) economic development, 4) family values and 5) leadership.

Challengers seek judgeship, schoolposts

April 30-May 2, 1994, The Union-Recorder, Milledgeville, GA (staff reports)

Announcement that funeral director and retired Army colonel Griffin, along with incumbent Baugh and Eatonton lawyer Marty Fierman, has qualified to run for District 25 seat. District includes Baldwin, Jones, Jasper, Putnam, Greene, Hancock, Warren and Taliaferro counties, and parts of Washington and Jefferson counties.

Senate candidates attack incumbent Baugh during forum

May 13, 1994, The Union-Recorder, Milledgeville, GA (Johnathan Burns, reporter)

Baugh a no-show at first political forum; Griffin and Fierman attack his perceived inefficacy. Fierman admits he made statement that Griffin would not get enough white votes to win; says Griffin's military background would make him better suited to serve as mayor of Milledgeville, not as senator of Georgia.

Yawn wins; Baugh, Griffin in runoff

July 20, 1994, The Union-Recorder, Milledgeville, GA (staff reports)

Front-page article. Chart shows that Baugh received 6,089 votes; Fierman, 3,480; and Griffin (listed third), 4,997.

Candidates spending hefty amounts in Senate race

(Date unknown) 1994, The Union-Recorder, Milledgeville (Don Schanche Jr., reporter)

After July 19 primary, and perhaps a week before Aug. 9 runoff, reporter gives summary of money Griffin and Baugh have received/invested in campaigning: Griffin, $22,081, for travel, office expenses and ads; Baugh, $33,559, mostly for ads.

(LETTER TO EDITOR): GRIFFIN OFFERS US HOPE FOR THE FUTURE

Aug. 6-8, 1994, (The Union Recorder, Milledgeville, GA (Willetta Stanley, letter writer, Milledgeville)

Praises Griffin for not merely highlighting problems in Baldwin County, but offering solutions—the only written solutions she has received from a candidate. Says Griffin's multiple achievements speaks volumes about his qualifications.

PUTNAM MAN TO RUN FOR 25TH DISTRICT SEAT AS WRITE-IN

Sept. 27, 1994, The Union-Recorder, Milledgeville, GA (staff reports)

Because Floyd Griffin won the Aug. 9 primary against Baugh, 41-year-old Putnam County pesticide contractor Alan Foster vows to run as a write-in candidate against Griffin.

WRITE-IN CANDIDATE PUTS WRINKLE INTO 11TH SENATORIAL DISTRICT RACE

Nov. 3, 1994, The Union-Recorder, Milledgeville, GA (Johnathan Burns, reporter)

While tradition suggests a guaranteed win for Griffin, who has no Republican opponent, Foster's presence puts pressure on Griffin to advocate for voter support in upcoming election. Foster, who supported Baugh's campaign, insists he can win.

BALDWIN VOTERS APPROVE BORROWING MONEY FOR LANDFILL AND JAIL PROJECTS, WHILE FLOYD GRIFFIN JR. COASTS TO VICTORY IN THE STATE SENATE

Nov. 9, 1994, The Union-Recorder, Milledgeville, GA (staff reports)

Announcement that Griffin wins 25th District seat; receives more than 10,000 votes to Foster's less than 600. Says he never considered Foster a threat. "I never thought it was a race. Americans thrive on individuals who work and work hard for what they get. That held true in my race."

GRIFFIN READY TO GET DOWN TO BUSINESS

(No date shown) The Union-Recorder, Milledgeville, GA (Johnathan Burns, reporter)

Reporter tells Baldwin County residents that although Sen.-elect Griffin has not yet been sworn in (an act to take place Jan. 9, 1995), he has already joined four Senate committees in order to fight on Baldwin's behalf: Health and Human Services, Governmental Operations, Higher Education, and Defense and Veterans Affairs.

AREA FRESHMEN ALREADY MAKING GREAT STRIDES

(No date shown) January 1995, The Macon Telegraph, Macon, GA (Nancy Badertscher, reporter)

Days before they are sworn in, reporter says that Macon Republican Sharon Falls and Sen. Griffin have already made history. Falls defeated long-time representative Denmark Groover and became the first female House member from Bibb County since the 1920s; and Griffin was in line to become the only sitting black legislator representing a majority-white district. Each candidate outlined plans for respective districts.

GRIFFIN BILL: '95 IS YEAR OF THE FAMILY

(Date unknown) The Macon Telegraph, Macon, GA (Rebecca Adams, reporter)

Senate unanimously approves a resolution Griffin brings to Senate floor, one declaring 1995 as the Year of the Family. Resolution emphasizes need to strengthen education, provide for the elderly, and combat crime and social problems with compassion. "It is the most important legislation I will sponsor in the time I remain in this body," the freshman senator says.

(Letter to Editor): Purpose of senator's visit to Union Point was to bring about healing, stability

March 10, 1995, The Macon Telegraph, Macon, GA (Sen. Floyd L. Griffin Jr., Atlanta)

In response to charges that he is a "liberal politician" who supports lawbreakers, Griffin clarifies his reason for visiting Union Point, GA, on Feb. 25, saying he was there to help heal "what has become a painful rift in a good, solid community." Says he is concerned about all citizens, black and white, who reside in his district.

Battle-weary legislators OK state budget

March 18, 1995, The Union-Recorder, Milledgeville, GA (news and wire reports)

Rep. Bobby Parham says that after Gov. Miller's proposed $7.8 million proposal to renovate the Old State Capitol building at Georgia Military College was whittled down to $1 million, Sen. Griffin persuaded fellow senators to boost it to $3.5 million. The Old Governor's Mansion at Georgia College will receive $300,000 for renovation.

GMC receives $3.5 million for renovations

March 18, 1995, The Macon Telegraph, Macon, GA (Cheryl Fincher, w/ Nancy Badertscher contributing)

Georgia Military College to receive $3.5 million for renovations, though some disapprove, saying the money should have gone to Baldwin County public schools. Griffin, who was director of facilities and engineering at GMC before becoming a senator, says the repairs at GMC are sorely needed.

Legislators call 1995 session successful one

March 23, 1995, The Union-Recorder, Milledgeville GA (Don Schanche Jr., reporter)

Griffin took lead in getting funds channeled to Milledgeville during his rookie season, especially after veteran Parham broke jaw in an accident. Among trophies are the renovation funds for GMC and the governor's mansion, as well as $100,000 for Oconee Area community mental-health services and $800,000 towards the building of a technical school. While Griffin recounts disappointment at having his student community-service idea become only a resolution and not a law, he was pleased that he passed the year-of-the-family resolution and a bill requiring write-in candidates to publish notices in each county in which they are running.

Privatization finds no fans...(rest of unable to be read)

Nov. 15, 1995, The Union-Recorder, Macon, GA (Don Schanche Jr., reporter)

Nearly 300 people, Griffin included, grill Larry Brockaway, assistant commissioner of the state Department of Veterans Services, about the state's plan to privatize the Georgia War Veterans Home. Brockaway unable to explain how the state would save the $8 million its claims it would save—without cutting back on personnel and services.

Griffin's bill would slow move to privatization

Nov. 30, 1995 (Paper unknown) (Staff and wire reports)

Griffin proposes bill that would require the governor to seek permission from the legislature if governor wants to hire private operators for jobs larger than janitorial services or grass cutting at the Capitol. Griffin also files a bill to temporarily halt the privatization of the 402-bed Georgia War Veterans Nursing Home in Milledgeville.

SENATORS HEAR PLEA FOR BILL TO REQUIRE PRIVATIZATION

February (no date shown) 1996, The Macon Telegraph, Macon, GA (Nancy Murray, reporter)

Beth Michael, president of the American Veterans Post No. 10 Auxiliary, pleads with Senate to support a bill prohibiting privatization of the veterans' home without legislative approval. Reps. of the Georgia State Employees Union, along with a group of veterans, prepare to go to court soon to seek an extension on the 120-day injunction issued Oct. 13 that barred the governor from proceeding forward with plans to privatize.

PRIVATIZATION FOES LOSE FIRST BATTLE

Feb. 16, 1996, The Union-Recorder, Milledgeville, GA (staff and wire reports)

The Senate agrees to let private interests run three new Georgia prisons, as well as the Georgia War Veterans Home in Milledgeville. Griffin vows to keep fighting.

GRIFFIN BLASTS PANEL FOR REFUSAL TO LISTEN

June 8, 1996, The Macon Telegraph (Nancy Badertscher, reporter)

Griffin displeased that the Fiscal Affairs Subcommittee did not allow him to address the committee before it took the final step needed to allow a private company to assume management of the veterans' home, a change scheduled for July 1.

PART II: 1997-2000—SENATOR AND LT. GOV. HOPEFUL RUN FOR LT. GOVERNOR

STATE SENATOR FLOYD GRIFFIN TO RUN FOR LIEUTENANT GOVERNOR

May 9, 1997, The Herald-Journal, Greensboro, GA (Staff reports)

Griffin announces intent to run for the higher office; says he will make official announcement on his birthday, May 24. Greene County included under his four-year senatorial reign.

GRIFFIN OPENS CAMPAIGN

May 27, 1997, The Union-Recorder, Milledgeville, GA (Don Schanche Jr., reporter)

Favorable report about Griffin's lieutenant-governor announcement made at current and former state capitols.

SENATOR GRIFFIN TO HEAD DAIRY STUDY PANEL

June 13, 1997, The Union-Recorder, Milledgeville, GA (staff reports)

Lt. Gov. Pierre Howard appoints Griffin to head the Georgia Dairy Production Study Committee, the purpose of which is to study "efforts to foster long-term viability of the industry and ways to improve university research."

PANEL TO STUDY STATE LAND HOLDINGS IN BALDWIN COUNTY

June 18, 1997, The Union-Recorder, Milledgeville, GA (Don Schanche Jr., reporter)

Griffin to chair panel to consider how to sell some of the more than 8,000 acres of land the state owns in Baldwin County.

GRIFFIN 'IN SYNC' WITH DEMOCRATIC LEADERSHIP

Dec. 17, 1997, The Union-Recorder, Milledgeville, GA (staff reports)

Griffin says he likes Democratic legislative priorities—parole elimination, $205 million income-tax cut, and privatization of municipal water systems that don't meet environmental standards—but says he needs to investigate them more.

STATE MINIMUM WAGE LAW PROBABLY COVERS FEW

Jan. 7, 1998, The Union-Recorder, Milledgeville, GA (Don Schanche Jr., reporter)

Sen. Griffin begins that week a statewide campaign to raise Georgia's minimum wage from $3.25/hr. to the federal minimum of $5.15.

GRIFFIN NAMED TO CHAIR SENATE PANEL

Jan. 13, 1998, The Union-Recorder, Milledgeville, GA (staff reports)

Lt. Gov. Pierre Howard appoints Sen. Griffin to head the Interstate Cooperation Committee, which deals with bills that relate to interstate agreements. Griffin replaces resigning Ralph David Abernathy III, who was disciplined by Senate after authorities fined Abernathy for marijuana possession.

GRIFFIN'S PLAN ADVANCES STATE PROPERTY SALE

Feb. 3, 1998, The Union-Recorder, Milledgeville, GA (Don Schanche Jr., reporter)

Senate approves Griffin's legislation to sell 72 state-owned houses and three tracts of land. Results are part of the investigation made by the state-property commission Griffin chaired in 1997.

GEORGIA WOULD JOIN SOUTHERN DAIRY GROUP UNDER NEW SENATE BILL

Feb. 4, 1998, The Union-Recorder, Milledgeville, GA (Don Schanche Jr., reporter)

Griffin gets Senate to pass a bill he sponsored that would make Georgia a member of the Southern Dairy Compact Commission, which can set a minimum price that Georgia's dairy farmers will set for their milk. Bill designed to help dairy farmers make a profit. Bill moves on to the House for its approval.

MILK PRICE SUPPORTS ENDORSED BY SENATE

Feb. 4, 1998, The Atlanta Journal-Constitution (staff reports)

Senate overwhelmingly passes dairy-compact bill. Article identifies Sen. Griffin as sponsor of the bill "that would allow Georgia to put representatives on a commission that sets minimum milk production prices for the region."

SENATE PASSES BUDGET BILL LADEN WITH PORK

Feb. 13, 1998, The Union-Recorder, Milledgeville, GA (wire and staff reports)

Announcement of bill, easily passed in Senate, that benefits local projects, including improvements of Milledgeville's Boys & Girls Club, Rape Crisis Center, and the architecturally valuable Griffin-Baugh Cottage that was donated by Sen. Griffin's father.

GRIFFIN EFFORT TO HIKE STATE MINIMUM WAGE SHOT DOWN

Feb. 14, 1998, The Macon Telegraph, Macon, GA (Tony Heffernan, reporter)

Announcement includes Griffin's appeal to legislators to reconsider their vote, as well as comments of opponents who dispute the existence of below-federal-minimum-wage workers in Georgia.

SENATE PASSES 'COVENANT' MARRIAGE BILL

Feb. 21, 1998, The Macon Telegraph, Macon, GA (Tony Heffernan, reporter)

Griffin opposes Pam Glanton's bill on the basis that it would unduly involve government in people's private lives. He criticized his colleagues for wanting government involvement only "when it's convenient."

SENATE VOTES TO HONOR PARHAM

(Date not known) The Macon Telegraph, Macon, GA (Tony Heffernan, reporter)

Griffin's resolution to name the kitchen at Milledgeville's Central State Hospital after Rep.

Bobby Parham passes the Senate 45-0.

LAWMAKERS FRIENDLY TO DAIRY INDUSTRY PUSH FOR COMPACT

(Date not listed, but likely Feb. 25th) 1998, The Macon Telegraph, Macon, GA (Tony Heffernan, reporter)

Griffin leads a group of some 20 dairy farmers and influential Georgia agricultural leaders at a news conference held at the Capitol in Atlanta. All want the dairy-compact legislation passed.

SENATE OKS TAX BREAKS FOR FARMERS

March 10, 1998, The Macon Telegraph, Macon, GA (Tony Heffernan, reporter)

A bill introduced by Griffin, and augmented by others, unanimously passes Senate. Bill exempts from property state taxes virtually all livestock and crops raised on family farms.

LAWMAKERS OK COMPACT FOR DAIRY FARMERS

March 14, 1998, The Macon Telegraph, Macon, GA (Tony Heffernan, reporter)

The House passed Griffin's bill 130-44 despite Republicans' concerns that it will lead to higher milk prices.

LIEUTENANT GOVERNOR'S RACE ANYONE'S TO WIN

March 31, 1998, The Atlanta Journal-Constitution (Tom Baxter, "On Politics")

Considers the diversity in the lieutenant governor's race but says that Griffin's name might work against him—it doesn't immediately identify him as African American—nor does he have the advertising money needed to let vast numbers of black Georgia voters see who he is.

MILLER VETOES DAIRY COMPACT

April 24, 1998, The Macon Telegraph, Macon, GA (Cheryl Fincher, reporter)

Griffin and others puzzled by Gov. Zell Miller's veto of bill. "This veto is potentially devastating for our dairy industry," says Griffin. "If the governor felt the bill was unconstitutional, let someone test it in the court."

GRIFFIN CONCERNED ABOUT 'OVERREACTION' TO NUWABIANS

May 8, 1998, The Union-Recorder, Milledgeville, GA (Don Schanche Jr., reporter)

Griffin meets with Putnam County Sheriff Howard Sills to discuss contention between Sills and Dr. Malachi York's Nuwabian Nation of Moors, located in Putnam. Griffin states in article that he visited the Nuwabians twice—once, unexpectedly—and found no cause for alarm. Says he wants the sheriff to treat Moors fairly and according to constitutional laws.

LT. GOV. CANDIDATE MAKES EDUCATION #1

May 21-22, 1998, The Atlanta Daily World (staff reports)

Griffin tells reporter that he intends to adequately compensate Georgia teachers, train them technologically, and empower them to take control of their classrooms.

STATEWIDE BLACK OFFICE-SEEKERS COURT WHITE VOTES

June 7, 1998, The Albany Herald, Albany, GA (Associated Press)

Griffin one of eight blacks seeking lieutenant-governor seat. Quoted as saying that whites have received him well, admitting they are voting, for the first time, for a black and that their forefathers "are rolling over in their graves" because of it.

Lt. Governor hopefuls take gloves off

June 25, 1998, The Albany Herald, Albany, GA (Associated Press)

During first televised debate between nine candidates, held in Savannah, Griffin roundly criticizes Mark Taylor for using cocaine in the past and says that Taylor should withdraw from the lieutenant governor's race because of it.

Lewis endorses Griffin for lieutenant governor

July 1, 1998, The Macon Telegraph, Macon, GA (staff reports)

U.S. Rep John Lewis calls Griffin "one of the most important Democratic leaders in Georgia and in America" and says that Georgia needs Griffin's leadership and vision.

Griffin campaign focuses on Atlanta

July 1, 1998, The Macon Telegraph, Macon, GA (R.J. Walker, reporter)

Griffin touts himself as the only candidate in race with a definitive educational plan—his includes using retired military personnel to improve student discipline. Says Georgia needs a lieutenant governor from Middle Georgia.

Floyd Griffin: Milledgeville Democrat

focusing on education

July 7, 1998, The Atlanta Journal-Constitution (Charmagne Helton, reporter)

Portrait of Griffin, a rural Georgia politician in leather cowboy boots and a pinstriped suit—and brown skin—who continues to hawk his education-based platform with less than a third of the campaign funds his opponents possess. Funding is low, the article says, despite Griffin's endorsements from some of Georgia's highest-ranking black officials.

Lieutenant governor's race crowded, wide open

July 14, 1998, The Macon Telegraph, Macon, GA (Matthew I. Pinzur, reporter)

Contrasts current diverse race with past Zell Miller-led Georgia pool of leaders. Griffin praised as only candidate to publish a comprehensive plan for education.

AFTER LT. GOVERNOR'S RACE

Griffin leaves Senate with no regrets

Jan. 9-11,1999, The Union-Recorder, Milledgeville, GA (Don Schanche Jr., reporter)

Brief, favorable recap of Griffin's achievements as he prepares to relinquish his seat to Faye Smith. Served two terms, brought much grant money to Milledgeville, looking forward to working with funeral home—but does not rule out political service.

Barnes gives state dairy farmers a boost

May 4, 1999, The Macon Telegraph, Macon, GA (Nancy Badertscher, reporter)

Announcement of Gov. Roy Barnes' approval of the legislation that would allow Georgia's dairy farmers to set a minimum price for milk. Mentions former Sen. Griffin as chair of the legislative study committee that highlighted the dramatic decline in the number of Georgia dairy farmers (but does not credit Griffin with authoring the legislation that helped the farmers).

(Letter to Editor): Former candidate criticizes Griffin

Sept. 23, 1999 (Likely, The Union-Recorder, Milledgeville, GA.) (Al R. Hudson, letter writer, Haddock, GA)

Finds Griffin's decision to run again a ludicrous one; says Griffin created a poor track record in the Senate; disagrees with Griffin's criticizing the successor he selected as his replacement.

GRIFFIN WANTS TO RETURN TO GEORGIA SENATE

Jan. 15, 2000, The Macon Telegraph, Macon, GA (Rob Peecher, reporter)

After serving two terms and then giving up his seat two years earlier to run for lieutenant governor, Griffin announces he has decided to run again for the District 25 Senate seat held by Faye Smith.

MACON'S MAYOR ENDORSES GRIFFIN

May 27-29, 2000, The Union-Recorder, Milledgeville, GA (staff reports)

Macon Mayor C. Jack Ellis, speaking at a campaign fundraiser at Baldwin High School, encourages audience to vote for Griffin because he "doesn't play racial politics. If you're right, he's with you," Ellis, who is African American, said. "If you're wrong, he's not with you."

FOUR BATTLE FROM TWO PARTIES IN SENATE RACE

June 23, 2000, The Union-Recorder, Milledgeville, GA (Jennifer Fowler, reporter)

Griffin and incumbent Smith battle for the Democratic nod for the Senate seat, while Johnny Grant III and Susan Olszewski vie for the Republican candidacy.

PART III: 2001-2006—MAYOR AND BEYOND

MAYORAL OFFICE

GRIFFIN ANNOUNCES MAYORAL PLANS

Sept. 4, 2001, The Union-Recorder, Milledgeville, GA (Jennifer James, reporter)

Hundreds meet in the rain at Walter B. Williams Jr. Park to support Griffin as he announces his intent to run for mayor of Milledgeville. Griffin promises to hire a city administrator, reorganize the city government so that it will run efficiently, and host "dialogue nights" with citizens who want to voice their concerns about community affairs. Also running in the upcoming election is the incumbent, Johnny Grant Jr., and resident Richard Bentley.

(LETTER TO EDITOR): READER APPRECIATES CANDIDATE MAKING HER, OTHERS FEEL WELCOME

Sept. 20, 2001, The Union-Recorder, Milledgeville, GA. (C. Gratton, letter writer, Milledgeville)

Writer encouraged by friendly attitude of Griffin and his campaign committee at the rainy Labor Day picnic, as well as by Griffin's rousing speech, in which he promises to become a leader who includes citizens in decision making and unifies the community.

RUNOFF SET FOR MILLEDGEVILLE

Nov. 7, 2001, The Macon Telegraph, Macon, GA (Rob Peecher, reporter)

Griffin and insurance-agency owner Richard Bentley emerge from a three-way race with incumbent Johnny Grant Jr. Griffin gets 1,276 votes; Bentley, 773; and Grant, 690. Griffin needed 1,370 votes to avoid a runoff.

THE VOTES ARE IN: GRIFFIN BY 21

Nov. 28, 2001, The Union-Recorder (Jennifer Copeland, reporter)

Griffin receives 1,521 votes to Bentley's 1,500 to win the election but is disappointed by low marginal turnout. Reporter discusses Bentley's reaction to results and examines past close victories and city voting patterns.

21 VOTES—GRIFFIN WINS MAYOR

November (date not seen) 2001, The Baldwin Bulletin, Milledgeville, GA (Pam Beer, editor)

Griffin credits Beverly Calhoun with helping to bring in 214 absentee ballots for him

(Bentley received 88). At the victory celebration, Griffin promises to have an inclusive, multi-racial administration, and his wife Nathalie thanked God for the victory.

MAYOR ANNOUNCES APPOINTMENTS;
NAMES NEW POLICE CHIEF

Jan. 3, 2002, The Union-Recorder, Milledgeville, GA (Jennifer Copeland, reporter)

Griffin appoints Woodrow Blue, former deputy chief of the city's police department, as interim police chief, and former Chief Fred Hayes as city marshal. Blue is black; Hayes is white.

(LETTER TO EDITOR): READER FEELS MANAGER IN BEST INTEREST OF CITY

Oct. 17, 2002, The Baldwin Bulletin, Milledgeville, GA. (Richard Bentley, letter writer, Milledgeville)

Applauds city council for arriving at the same conclusion Bentley promoted during last mayoral election—that Milledgeville would run better with a city manager. Says such a setup would unify mayor and council and strengthen them as a body. Says other Georgia cities of comparable size have done so, with positive results, so the community should support the council's decision to create a manager position.

SOCIAL SECURITY HEARINGS TO TAKE PLACE HERE

July 7, 2004, The Union-Recorder, Milledgeville, GA (Joseph Tkacik, reporter)

Patti Patterson, deputy regional communications director for the Social Security Administration, and Regional Chief Judge Ollie Garmon thank Mayor Griffin for working with them to make it possible for Milledgeville residents to have their Social Security appeals heard in Milledgeville, instead of having to do so in Atlanta.

(LETTER TO EDITOR): CITIZEN UNHAPPY OVER MAYOR'S ACTIONS

July 15, 2004, The Baldwin Bulletin, Milledgeville, GA. (Peter J. Boylan, letter writer, Milledgeville)

Says that Griffin, in Boylan's opinion, is casting Milledgeville in a bad light by the lawsuits Griffin has filed against city council and by Griffin's refusal to consider others' points of view in running the city.

MILLEDGEVILLE IN 'TOUGH SITUATION'

Aug. 8, 2004, The Macon Telegraph, Macon, GA (Gary Tanner, reporter)

Milledgeville City Councilman Ken Vance says that Griffin's lawsuits, which argue that voters were betrayed by the change to a weak-mayor form of government, contribute to an uneasy working relationship between Griffin and the city council. The pending court appearances before state and local judges, Griffin's request that the GBI investigate council members, and failed attempts on the part of Griffin supporters to remove some of the council members all contribute, Vance says, to the stiff business relationship between mayor and council.

SOME MILLEDGEVILLE LEADERS WANT TIME TO STUDY FINALISTS

Aug. 23, 2004, The Macon Telegraph, Macon, GA (Gary Tanner, reporter)

Investigation reveals problems in the career backgrounds of the three Milledgeville city-manager finalists, especially Ron Rabun, who left the city of Griffin with a $6.5 million deficit, says Griffin Mayor Cynthia Ward. However, a former Griffin commissioner, Tom Perdue, says Rabun had an excellent and unblemished record.

RABUN SELECTED AS CITY MANAGER

August (No date) 2004, The Baldwin Bulletin, Milledgeville, GA (Pam Beer, editor)

The city council votes to approve Ron Rabun as its choice for city manager. Griffin, who has opposed the city-manager installation, declines to attend the meeting (appointing Mayor pro-tem Ken Vance to chair). Council members Vance, Richard Hudson, Dennette O. Jackson and Jeanette Walden vote yes for Rabun, while Richard "Boo" Mullins vote against the selection because he thinks the council should more thoroughly investigate Rabun's background before hiring him. Walden says her investigation led to more praise than negative comments about Walden; also, she found him to have operated "well within" the budget. Council member Denese Shinholster, not a staunch Rabun supporter, is absent due to a death in the family.

City loses manager candidate to S.C. county

Aug. 28-30, 2004, The Union-Recorder, Milledgeville, GA (Payton Towns III, reporter)

Three days after Milledgeville City Council selects Ron Rabun to become city manager, he signs a contract to become county administrator for Oconee County, South Carolina. Councilmen Vance and Hudson, who voted yes to appoint Rabun, claim they are not angered by Rabun's move to Oconee but support him.

It's back to square one for City Council

Sept. 4-6, 2004, The Union-Recorder, Milledgeville, GA (editorial)

Says that city council's appointment of Barry Jarrett as acting city manager means the council is no closer now to finding a permanent manager than it was at the start of its search. Says Griffin had the right idea when he suggested, after Rabun's cut and run, that council should consider its two remaining candidates or start all over. Says Griffin can take a moment to snicker at council's fumbling.

GMC gives up its city water subsidy in pre-emptive move

September (no date) 2004, The Baldwin Bulletin, Milledgeville, GA (Pam Beer, editor)

Mayor Griffin asks the city's utilities department to look into a $500 monthly credit given to Georgia Military College, apparently with the intention of having the arrangement terminated. However, Peter Boylan, GMC president, voluntarily ends the subsidy, at the same time citing all the contributions GMC makes to Baldwin County. Some accuse Griffin of retaliating because of Boylan's July letter to the editor that criticized Griffin, but the mayor says he was bothered by the subsidy before Boylan wrote the letter.

Housing project for elderly adults approved

Sept. 29, 2004, The Union-Recorder, Milledgeville, GA (Payton Towns III, reporter)

One of Griffin's 2003 initiatives finally wins approval from the Department of Community Affairs: Pecan Hills, a 54-unit affordable-housing development for the independent elderly.

Mayor challenges city council move to honor Parham

Sept. 30, 2004, The Baldwin Bulletin, Milledgeville, GA (Pam Beer, editor)

Mayor Griffin objects to the timing—in the midst of an election year—for a City Council resolution to honor State Rep. Bobby Parham for his 29 years of service. Griffin says he respects Parham but thinks council should wait until after the representative's reelection campaign is over so that it won't appear they are endorsing him.

Help wanted (again)

Oct. 7, 2004, The Baldwin Bulletin, Milledgeville, GA (Pam Beer, editor)

Says Milledgeville can reinstate its help wanted sign in the window of the city-manager's office. Michael Nettles, who signed a contract to become Milledgeville city manager after council unanimously selected him on Sept. 14, changes his mind and decides to remain at his job as city administrator of Altus, Okla. Councilman Ken Vance says he thinks Nettles retreated because he did not want Griffin and other opponents of the governmental change probing into his background.

(LETTER TO EDITOR): THOSE WHO ARE IN POLITICS SHOULD LOOK BEFORE THEY LEAP

Oct. 23, 2004 (Paper not shown) (Ann Waller, letter writer, Milledgeville, GA)

Chides city council for passing resolution to honor Bobby Parham just a few weeks before his reelection campaign. Says council members, when serving in their public roles, should do a better job of hiding their personal political preferences.

MAYOR, COUNCIL AT ODDS ABOUT MEETING TO DISCUSS CITY MANAGER

Oct. 27, 2004, The Union-Recorder, Milledgeville, GA (Payton Towns III, reporter)

Bitter meeting between council and mayor, with Councilmen Vance and Hudson blaming Griffin's lawsuits and "undermining" efforts for the council's failure to secure a city manager, and with Griffin charging the council with violating the charter in calling its own committee-of-the-whole meeting.

A SKUNK BY ANY OTHER SMELL WOULD STINK AS MUCH

Nov. 13-15, 2004 (Probably The Union-Recorder, Milledgeville, GA) (editorial)

Editor blames the city council, and not Mayor Griffin, for the failure to find a city manager.

JUDGE ASKS LAWYERS FOR PROPOSED ORDERS IN MAYOR, COUNCIL LAWSUITS

Dec. 1, 2004, The Union-Recorder, Milledgeville, GA (Payton Towns III, reporter)

Some 50 people attended the hearing as attorneys for Mayor Griffin and for the city present their cases before Baldwin County Superior Court Judge William Towson Sr. Judge gives both sides 10 days to submit orders about Griffin's lawsuits. Griffin's primary lawsuit charges that the Milledgeville change of government was unconstitutional; his second requests clarification about who has authority to appoint a sergeant-at-arms for city-council meetings.

MAYOR'S LAWSUIT GETS ITS DAY IN SUPERIOR COURT

Dec. 2, 2004, The Baldwin Bulletin, Milledgeville, GA (Pam Beer, editor)

Appearing before Judge William Towson Sr., Griffin's attorney, James E. Voyles, argues that when the 2003 General Assembly approved a change of Milledgeville government in the midst of Griffin's term, it stripped him of all but ceremonially duty and therefore violated a Georgia code that says an office cannot be abolished during the term of an office holder.

JUDGE RULES IN COUNCIL'S FAVOR IN LAWSUITS; MAYOR PLANS TO APPEAL.

Dec. 18-20, 2004, The Union-Recorder, Milledgeville, GA (Payton Towns III, reporter)

Dublin Judge William Towson rules that the "challenged legislation is not constitutionally flawed" and that Griffin's mayoral office was not abolished. Councilman Vance says that though Griffin has a right to appeal, he hopes Griffin does not waste more of the taxpayers' money by filing an appeal.

MAYOR, AGENCIES KICK OFF AFFORDABLE HOUSING PLAN

Jan. 14, 2005, The Union-Recorder, Milledgeville, GA (Amy H. Mullis, reporter)

Mayor Griffin and the City are working with local nonprofit agencies and the Middle Georgia Regional Development Center to determine how to bring more affordable housing to Milledgeville. The city hopes to receive a Community Home Improvement Program grant this year.

CITY TO PILOT SAFETY PROGRAM FOR CHILDREN

Jan. 26, 2005, The Union-Recorder, Milledgeville, GA (Amy H. Mullis, reporter)

Griffin announces at city-council meeting that the Georgia Conference of Black Mayors has selected Milledgeville as one of five Georgia cities to pilot the Hand in Hand with Children: Guiding and Protecting program, which will photograph and fingerprint children and link their information with the National Center for Missing and Exploited Children.

GEORGIA SUPREME COURT TO HEAR MAYOR'S SUIT IN APRIL

Feb. 3, 2005, The Baldwin Bulletin, Milledgeville, GA (Pam Beer, editor)

Griffin pleased and optimistic about the Georgia Supreme Court's decision to hear his suit filed against the city council. Ken Vance thinks his side will prevail because of the Justice Department's pre-approval of the council's charter change.

JUDGE RULES FOR CITY IN MAYOR'S SUIT

February (No date) 2005, The Union-Recorder (Payton Towns III, reporter)

Federal Judge Duross Fitzpatrick of the U.S. District Court for the Middle District of Georgia in Macon rules against Griffin in his lawsuit filed against Gov. Sonny Perdue, Faye Smith, Bobby Parham, and the six members of the Milledgeville City Council. Judge states that the coun NCTRCA cil did nothing wrong when it asked the General Assembly to change Milledgeville's city charter.

COURT DISMISSES MAYOR'S FEDERAL SUIT

May 19, 2005, The Union-Recorder, Milledgeville, GA (Keich Whicker, reporter)

Griffin lets the deadline pass for filing a Civil Appeals Statement, deciding not to pursue his lawsuit at the federal level but choosing instead to concentrate on the state suit.

MAYOR ENCOURAGES YES ON SPLOST

Sept. 10, 2005, The Union-Recorder, Milledgeville, GA (Keich Whicker, reporter)

Mayor Griffin encourages residents to vote for the SPLOST referendum, a single-penny tax that will ultimately bring $45 million dollars in funds for improving infrastructure, roads, and other factors related to public safety.

GRIFFIN NAMED TO NATIONAL BOARD

Dec. 21, 2006, The Baldwin Bulletin, Milledgeville, GA (staff reports)

The National Center for Missing and Exploited Children selects former mayor Griffin to serve on its board of directors. The NCMEC pilot program in Milledgeville, which Griffin introduced as mayor, became the national model.

Photo Gallery

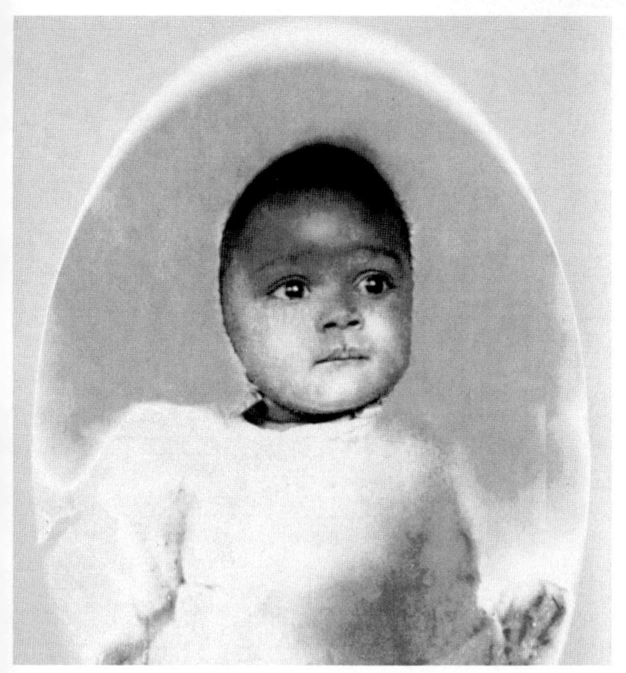

Cadet Captain Floyd L. Griffin, Jr.

Floyd L. Griffin, Jr., 1 year old.

7th grade, Floyd L. Griffin, Jr.

Captain Floyd L. Griffin, Jr. Company Commander.

Official Photo - Vietnam.

Company Staff NCO's - Vietnam, 1971.

Pilot and Flight Instructor
Cpt. Floyd L. Griffin, Jr.
227th ASH BN. -Vietnam.

Company Inspection, Vietnam.

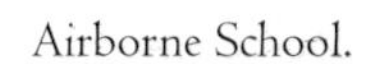

Airborne School.

THE UNITED STATES OF AMERICA

TO ALL WHO SHALL SEE THESE PRESENTS, GREETING:

THIS IS TO CERTIFY THAT
THE PRESIDENT OF THE UNITED STATES OF AMERICA
AUTHORIZED BY EXECUTIVE ORDER, 24 AUGUST 1962
HAS AWARDED

THE BRONZE STAR MEDAL

(SECOND OAK LEAF CLUSTER)

TO

CAPTAIN FLOYD L. GRIFFIN 254-70-4688 UNITED STATES ARMY CORPS OF ENGINEERS

FOR

MERITORIOUS ACHIEVEMENT
IN GROUND OPERATIONS AGAINST HOSTILE FORCES
IN THE REPUBLIC OF VIETNAM DURING THE PERIOD AUGUST 1970 TO JULY 1971
GIVEN UNDER MY HAND IN THE CITY OF WASHINGTON
THIS FIRST DAY OF JULY 19 71

KBCooper
K. B. COOPER
Brigadier General, USA

Stanley R. Resor
SECRETARY OF THE ARMY

Change of Command
92nd. Engineering
Battalion, Ft. Stewart, GA.

Winston- Salem State University Football team backfield with Coach Captain Floyd L. Griffin.

Timmy Newsome

Winston- Salem State University Football Coaching Highlights

Left: Randy Bolton. Right: Heavyweight Champion, Joe Frazier at home of Captain Floyd L. Griffin, Jr. Below: Players admiring the CIAA Championship Trophy.

Lt. Col. Floyd L. Griffin, Jr. with the Chaplin, 92nd. Engineering Battalion.

Presenting award to a soldier.

Colonel. Floyd L. Griffin, Jr. and Mrs. Nathalie Griffin host General Colin Powell, and his wife during a ceremony at aTuskegee University ROTC 2nd. Lt. Commissioning Program.

During a field exercise Lt. Colonel Griffin, Commander, 92nd. Engineering Battalion with Major General H. Norman Schwarzkopf who was Commander of the 24th Infantry Division. He later became Commander in Chief of the U.S. Central Command during the Persian Gulf War.

Lt. Col. Griffin tries his hand at rug making during a visit to a Greek rug factory. This was part of the National War College trip to Athens Greece.

Setting with Lt. Col. Fred Black, a National War College classmate. We were in Athens Greece at the original Olympic Stadium.

Senator Floyd L. Griffin, Jr. with his grandson, Jamal and Leon Mitchell, campaign manager.

Giving a TV interview as a candidate for Lt. Governor of Georgia.

Senator Floyd L. Griffin, Jr. with Atty. Johnnie Cochran and Dr. Prather, President, Fort Valley State University.

Promotion to Colonel. Floyd L. Griffin, Jr. being pinned during ceremony by Mrs. Nathalie Griffin and Major General Charles Williams at The Pentagon.

Senator Griffin with civil rights legend and U.S. Representative John Lewis.

With U.S. Representative Sanford Bishop. (D - GA).

Mrs. Nathalie Griffin addresses news conference as Rep. Tyrone Brooks, Senator Griffin, Ms. Beverly Hill and others look on.

Senator Griffin with Ambassador Andrew Young.

Candidates for Governor and Lieutenant Governor of Georgia: State Representative Roy Barnes and Senator Floyd L. Griffin, Jr. Below left: A campaign endorsement from U.S. Rep. Cynthia Mckinney. Right:: Senator and Mrs. Griffin with Governor and Mrs. Zell Miller at Governor's Mansion.

Senator Griffin and U.S. Senator Max Cleland, D. -GA, both decorated Vietnam War veterans.

Below: Senator Griffin speaking from the well of the Georgia State Senate.

Senator Floyd L. Griffin, Jr. and Senator Mark Taylor qualifying to run for Lt. Governor.

Senator and Mrs. Floyd L. Griffin, Jr. and Mayor Jack Ellis, first Black Mayor of Macon, GA.

The Presidential Inaugural Committee
requests the honor of your presence
to attend and participate
in the
Inauguration of
William Jefferson Clinton
as
President of the United States of America
and
Albert Gore, Jr.
as
Vice President of the United States of America
on Monday, the twentieth of January
one thousand nine hundred and ninety-seven
in the City of Washington

First Lady Nathalie. Griffin fashionably attired for a special evening.

Below: Floyd L. Griffin, Jr. greeting Mrs. Emma Freeman, one of the pillars of the Milledgeville community who was in attendance at historic swearing in ceremony of Milledgeville, GA's first African American mayor.

FLOYD L. GRIFFIN

★ LIEUTENANT GOVERNOR ★

Post Office Box 1430 • 100 South Wilkinson • Milledgeville, Georgia 31061
Phone (912) 453-7724 • Fax (912) 453-7751 • e-mail: GriffinLtG@aol.com

Professor

Helicopter Pilot in Vietnam

College Football Coach

Husband

Father and Grandfather

Businessman and State Senator

"When the challenges of the state are ever-changing, it is only natural to elect a Lt. Governor who has solved problems from battlefields to playing fields, from classrooms to boardrooms and from the Pentagon to the state Senate."

Floyd L. Griffin

® GCU 753M

Floyd L. Griffin, Jr. speaking at an ecumentical service the evening before the mayor's swearing in ceremony at the Chapel of All Faiths at Central State Hospital, Milledgeville, GA. Below: Receiving election results of victory as Mayor of the City of Milledgeville, GA. Felix Jones, holding the mic̈, Commisioner Geneva Davis and 1st. Lady Nathalie Griffin celebrate the news.

Mayor Floyd L. Griffin, Jr. being sworn in by Supreme Court Justice Hugh Thompson.

Mayor Floyd L. Griffin, Jr. speaking to the attendees of the Black Heritage gathering during Milledgeville's Dr. Martin Luther King, Jr. Celebration.

Below: Rev. Al Sharpton and President of New York Chapter, 100 Black Men at Gala in New York.

Senator Floyd L. Griffin, Jr. being sworn in by Supreme Court Justice Hugh Thompson.

Two History Makers Awardees. Mayor Floyd L. Griffin, Jr. pictured with Mr. Robert T. Church, Sr. in Chicago, IL.

Senator Floyd L. Griffin, Jr. with the Olympic Torch in Milledgeville, GA.

Senator Floyd L. Griffin, Jr. and retired U.S. Army Lt. Col. Ted Nell, a 30 year friend.

Senator Floyd L. Griffin, Jr. and Lt. Governor Pierre Howard.

Below: Senator Floyd L. Griffin, Jr., left; Senator Ralph Abernathy, (2nd. row, left; U.S. Rep. David Scott, U.S. Rep. Sanford Bishop, Senator Charles Walker; top; Senator Ed Harberson, Lt. Gov. Pierre Howard and Senator Robert Brown.

Senator Floyd L. Griffin, Jr. pictured above with members and guests at the Georgia State Capitol.

Right: At the GA State Senate with lifelong friend Major (Rt.) Charles McCampbell.

Press Conference announcing my run for Lt. Governor. Pictured with Fulton Co. Commissioner Michael Hightower, Ambassador Andrew Young, Honorary Chair of my election and his wife, Carolyn. Attorney Thomas Cuffie and Rep. Tyrone Brooks.

Pictured with Mr and Mrs. Willie Fluellen and Lt. Gov. Pierre Howard at the Georgia State Capitol.

Senator Floyd L. Griffin, Jr. and Senator George Hooks of Americus, GA.

With U.S. Representative David Scott at the Georgia State Capitol.

Mayor Floyd L. Griffin, Jr., National Board member, National Center for Missing & Exploited Children along with and Mr. Herb Jones, Vice President of the organization. They are also celebrated Tuskegee Institute (University) graduates and were classmates.

National Center for Missing & Exploited Children

Mission

The National Center for Missing & Exploited Children's® (NCMEC) mission is to help prevent child abduction and sexual exploitation; help find missing children; and assist victims of child abduction and sexual exploitation, their families, and the professionals who serve them.

NCMEC was established in 1984 as a private, nonprofit 501(c)(3) organization to provide services nationwide for families and professionals in the prevention of abducted, endangered, and sexually exploited children.

Robbie Calloway, National Board Member of National Center for Missing & Exploited Children, Alexandria, VA., Ernie Allen, President and CEO of the organization and National Board Member Mayor Floyd L. Griffin, Jr.

Below: Macon, GA Mayor Jack Ellis, Vice President Al Gore and Senator Floyd L. Griffin.

Highlights of the Milledgeville, GA Bi-Centennial Ball featuring Governor Sonny Purdue.

At Milledgeville, Ga Bi-Centennial Ball Mayor Floyd L. Griffin, Jr. is presented the State of Georgia's special proclaimation by Governor Sonny Perdue as Mrs. Perdue and Congressman Jim Marshall-Macon, GA (far left) and Chairman-Baldwin County Board of Commissions Ace Parker look on.

The First Lady of Milledgeville, GA, Mrs. Nathalie Huffman Griffin.

Floyd L. Griffin, in office during 1st. campaign for the senate.

Mayor Griffin playing softball.

Family

Senator and Mrs. Floyd L. Griffin, Jr.

Mayor and Mrs. Nathalie Huffman Griffin with Mayor Griffin's History Makers' Award.

Father and mother pinning the Major oak leaf on son, Major Brian Griffin.

Family

Son, Eric Griffin and Family: wife: Susan, sons Jamal, Bakari and Zac; and daughter, AnnaGail.

Son, Brian Griffin and Family: wife: Terra, Braxton and Brandon (standing).

Family

Brother Toney W. Griffin and Family: wife: Barbara Cutts Griffin, son Toney Wyndero, and daughter, Tonisha D. Griffin.

Sister,
Delbra A. Griffin Waller

Delbra's son, my nephew, Wade Waller, III and wife, Miosoti D. Espinal -Waller baby, Adelaida R. Waller.

News article commemorating my parent's 60th wedding anniversary.

Mr. & Mrs. Floyd L. Griffin Sr.

Mr. and Mrs. Floyd L. Griffin Sr. celebrated their sixtieth wedding anniversary on Friday, September 13, 2002. A 60th anniversary celebration and his birthday occasion was held at the home of their son in Atlanta with their children, Mayor Floyd and Natalie Griffin, Toney and Barbara Griffin and Delbra Griffin Waller; grandchildren, Brian and Terra Griffin, Eric and Suzanne Griffin, Wyndero Griffin, Tonisha Griffin and Wade Waller III; and four great-grandchildren, Jamal Griffin, Bakari Griffin, Brandon Griffin and Braxton Griffin.

Mr. Griffin married the former Ruth Evans. They are the owners of Slater's Funeral Home, Inc. in Milledgeville.

Floyd L. Griffin, Sr., French Consul General Rene Ferge Marty and Mayor Floyd L. Griffin, Jr.

Family

Rev. Willie T. "Papa" Griffin, my grandfather.
He was a Pastor and operated his own business.

Hattie Taylor Evans and Johnnie Evans, my maternal grandparents.

Family

Mr. Gaston and Mrs. Charlotte Huffman of Birmingham, AL, Nathalie's parents. .
Celebrating their 55th wedding anniversary, October, 1990.

Family

Brian and Eric with mother and grandparents Gaston and Charlotte Huffman.

Patricia Huffman Wilson, my sister-in-law, Nathalie's sister.

Right Page:

Floyd L. Griffin Sr. and Ruth Evans Griffin with Nathalie.

Below: Floyd, Sr., Senator, Nathalie, Toney Griffin, Delbra Griffin Waller. Seated: Mother, Ruth Evans Griffin, Willie Mae Knox, and Aunt Alma Speights.

Family

Family

Bennie Evans (uncle)

Holding my youngest family member, great neice Adelaida R. Waller.

Family

Griffin family voting event. The Honorable Floyd L. Griffin, Jr., sister Delbra Griffin Waller and brother Toney Griffin escort their mother Ruth Evans Griffin to the voting polls that she may cast her vote for Senator Barack Obama as the Democratic candidate for President. of the United States. (Nov. 2008)

Sigma Pi Phi Fraternity
Beta Chi Boule

Ft. Valley, Georgia

Floyd L. Griffin, Jr. (seated first row, far right) is an Archon and Nathalie Griffin (Standing, third from left) is an Archousa in the Beta Chi Boule of Sigma Pi Phi Fraternity. Pictured on the opposite page are its Archon and their Archousai. Sigma Pi Phi Fraternity, also known as the Boule, is the first Greek-letter fraternity to be founded by African American men. Significantly, unlike the other African American Greek -letter organizations, its members already have received college and professional degrees at the time of their induction. The fraternity's insignia is the Sphinx.

From the beginning, Sigma Pi Phi Fraternity was a learned society, a social fraternity and an advancement organization, albeit a quiet one. As well, the fraternity believed absolutely in the equality of standing of its members and insisted that anyone who was eligible for membership was eligible and qualified for leadership. The founders were so certain of this fact that the fraternity selected its officers by lot, a custom that continued for the most senior officer until 1970.

In the late 1990s and the beginnings of the new century the Boulé undertook two other initiatives that would underpin the fraternity's successful move into its second century. During the terms of Grand Sire Archons Anthony Hall, Eddie Williams and Thomas Shropshire, the Grand Boulé established a Public Policy Committee and initiated a study that resulted in a fraternity-wide strategic plan. At one hundred years of age, the Grand Boulé of Sigma Pi Phi Fraternity is poised and well prepared for another century of service.

Sigma Pi Phi Fraternity
Beta Chi Boule

Ft. Valley, Georgia

Archons

Archousai

Three History Makers:

The Presidential Inaugural Committee

requests the honor of your presence

to attend and participate

in the

Inauguration of

Barack H. Obama

as President of the United States of America

and

Joseph R. Biden, Jr.

as Vice President of the United States of America

on Tuesday, the twentieth of January

two thousand and nine

in the City of Washington